ROCKET MEN

ROCKET MEN

Tales From The Vicarage

Volume Six
by Oliver Phillips and Mike Walters

TALES FROM

www.talesfrom.com

First published in Great Britain in 2017
by Tales From

Printed and bound by Page Bros Ltd

Visual design and photography by www.stonecreativedesign.com
Cover typography and additional design by Steve Leard

ISBN 978-0-9932381-6-1

Tales From Ltd
107 Jupiter Drive, Hemel Hempstead, Herts HP2 5NU
Registered company number: 9082738

www.talesfrom.com
info@talesfrom.com

ROCKET MEN

CONTENTS

FOREWORD

BY JOHN BARNES

I would not have missed my time at Watford – either for the success we enjoyed on the pitch or the people who helped to define me as a person – for all the world.

If I had my time again, I would not change a thing. If I had not played with those lads and for Graham Taylor as my manager I would not have become the footballer I was or the person I am now. We are all moulded as characters by certain passages in our lives, and I will always consider myself fortunate that I was recommended to Watford by a taxi driver who knew one of the club's scouts. I will always be thankful that Bertie Mee took up his scout's recommendation and reached an agreement that I would sign for Watford after my father invited him round to my parents' house to discuss it over a gin and tonic.

I didn't know that much about Watford, or their history, when I arrived at the club in 1981 and first set foot on the training ground at Stanmore. I had heard the whispers about a club on the rise, and they had already risen from obscurity to the second tier, or what is now the Championship. But when I look back, it was a marvellous achievement that a core of players went all the way from the old Fourth Division to second in the League behind the great Liverpool team of that era.

Steve Sherwood, Ross Jenkins, Luther Blissett and Ian Bolton's places in Watford's history are secure, but they were more than team-mates. They became my family. At 17 years old, I learned from the outset that each of them would always put the team above his individual talent or personal ambition to ensure we had each other's backs. Watford was the original family club, Graham Taylor was head of the family, and the team he built were like my brothers.

Graham took us to the heart of the local community, and the hearts of Watford supporters, like nobody else. He recognised these four Rocket Men were good people, and potentially great footballers, who would give everything to the cause, on and off the pitch. And under their guidance, I discovered how that connection made us better players – and better human beings.

I wasn't there at the start of Watford's rise, so I didn't witness how they had gone about playing the likes of Rochdale, Crewe Alexandra and Southend in the lower divisions. But every time Watford Football Club rose a level, their ability shone through. To go from one end of the football spectrum to indispensable players in the second-best team in the country was incredible. English football's landscape has changed so much in the last 30 years that their story is unlikely to be repeated elsewhere, so I am privileged to help recall and revisit it.

In modern football, there are examples of players who prosper on every step of the pyramid – like Jamie Vardy, all the way from non-League to winning the title with Leicester and gaining England recognition – but there are few parallels, if any, with the Watford side I joined, where a band of brothers stayed together through the divisions.

Steve Sherwood was a quiet hero. Often it was Watford's forwards who took the plaudits – and on one occasion I stole the headlines by scoring a hat-trick against Cardiff in the League Cup – but it was Steve who set us on the road to the quarter-finals by saving a penalty first; otherwise we would probably have fallen at the first hurdle.

Ian Bolton was known affectionately to his team-mates as 'Webby' because he walked out of the showers one day and one of the lads decided he looked like Captain Matt Webb, the first man to swim the English Channel. As well as being a wonderfully clean striker of the ball (and mark my words, his shooting at set pieces was like a sledgehammer), he was also the perfect host. Every Friday night before a home game, a group of young players – usually Nigel Callaghan, Steve Terry, Kenny Jackett and me – would go round his house to watch a video and his wife would make us a plate of chips. Happy days!

As far as I'm concerned, Ross Jenkins was good enough to play for England – and he can count himself unlucky that he missed out on an international career because we were blessed with a decent crop of strikers and he happened to be part of the same generation as Keegan, Francis and Woodcock. In another era, Ross might have won multiple caps because he was such an unselfish and intelligent player.

And of course, Luther was a shining light. Coming from Jamaica like me, we instantly shared a cultural connection . . . and his mum's goat curry was always a highlight! His partnership with Ross was feared by defences all over the country, he paved the way for younger black players like myself to prosper, and at Watford we felt loved and respected. Even when Manchester United came calling, Luther's love for the club who gave him his break in League football took him back to Vicarage Road after he had broadened his horizons at AC Milan.

When my father returned to Jamaica from his posting to London as a military attaché, my parents needed to know their teenage son would be in good hands, but they needn't have worried. I was lucky enough, and privileged, to stay behind in England, play my part in Watford's incredible journey and count Steve, Ian, Ross and Luther as team-mates, friends, extended family.

By the time I left the club in 1987, at the age of 23, I had enjoyed six years of first-team football, five years in the top flight and four years as an England international. I could not have asked for a better upbringing in the game, and I owe so much to a great manager and a group of players whose team ethic endures to this day.

When Graham Taylor passed away in January 2017, the turnout of ex-players at his funeral spoke volumes for the high regard in which he was held and the spirit of togetherness he fostered, whether we were defying the odds in football matches, joining the annual Pancake Day race around the pond at the top of the High Street, pushing over mountains of pennies in a pub on a Thursday night or enjoying the end-of-season cabaret at Baileys nightclub. There were so many familiar faces, generating the warmth and camaraderie of old times, that it felt like walking back into the dressing room 35 years ago.

This book is a tribute to the great servants of Watford Football Club who played in all four divisions under Graham's management, but effectively it is also a tribute to the boss himself. Graham Taylor was the Bill Shankly of Watford. He revolutionised the club and he made the people happy. He conceived a perfect storm of cup shocks, attacking football and community spirit. And he assembled a very, very good team.

The memories I have of those times are stronger because of our achievements, and I was very fortunate that my football education at Vicarage Road provided such a sound platform for me to sustain the next chapter of my career at Liverpool. Could a 17-year-old boy have gone straight into the first-team squad at Anfield, and handled the accolades of being a kid with star potential, without learning the ropes first? I doubt it very much. I owe Graham Taylor, the players and the whole club a debt of gratitude. Watford brought me up the right way and helped to define me both as a footballer and as a person.

To those of you who saw the Rocket Men play, I hope their stories will remind you how integral they were to a fantastic story. Much as I admired their talents as team-mates, most of all I will always value them as good people.

And to 'Shirley', 'Webby', Ross and Luther – great players, great friends – I can only repeat what I felt when I made my Liverpool debut: 'You paved the way. You helped to make it happen. Thank you.'

John Barnes

INTRODUCTION

BY THE EDITOR

I t was a filthy Thursday lunchtime in January, slate-grey skies and raining knitting needles, when the dreadful news filtered through. Graham Taylor, the architect of Watford Football Club's magic-carpet ride from obscurity to eminence, had passed away suddenly at the age of 72.

For every supporter who lived through a decade of unimaginable excitement between 1977-87, his death forced us to reflect that seldom, if ever, has a single man's influence coloured so many lives – on and off the pitch – and transformed a whole town's outlook.

On the incredible journey across those ten years, Taylor delivered three promotions, an FA Cup final, two other major semi-finals, five more quarter-finals and European football – including arguably the single greatest result in the club's history: winning 3-1 in Bulgaria against Levski Spartak of Sofia after being held 1-1 at home in the first leg.

But in an age of hooligan excess, Taylor's greatest triumph – by far his greatest achievement – was to establish Watford as an oasis of safe, inclusive family entertainment. Where other clubs penned supporters in cages, the fences never went up at Vicarage Road, and Taylor even raised £35,000 towards the family terrace – no adults admitted unless accompanied by a responsible child – by running the London Marathon in 1983.

So when the club was plunged into mourning, and his family showed superhuman dignity to attend the home game with Middlesbrough 48 hours later, it didn't just feel like a death at English football's first true family club; it felt like a death in the family.

In the hearts and minds of Watford supporters, Taylor's legend will never be vanquished, but now here – as a celebration of his inspirational leadership – the players have their say. *Rocket Men* charts the Hornets' rise through the eyes of the four foot soldiers who played in all four divisions of the club's astonishing climb.

Steve Sherwood was the goalkeeper who saw it all: promotions, Europe, FA Cup final, the lot. His unbroken service straddled the Golden Boys' golden decade under Taylor, and his contribution was as priceless as it was often underrated beyond Vicarage Road.

Ian Bolton, one of Taylor's first signings for Watford, cost just £12,500 and turned out to be a Rembrandt at a boot sale. Those raking passes from centre-back may have been damned with faint praise as long balls by outsiders with agendas, but he was a pivotal influence on the club's success.

Luther Blissett made more appearances and scored more goals for the Hornets than anyone in the club's history. Revered as Watford's favourite son, he was also their first player to win England caps at senior international level and he became, quite simply, the poster boy for the unfettered joy of Taylor's regime.

And Ross Jenkins, lampooned and harpooned during an uncertain start at Vicarage Road, forged a dynamic double act with Blissett. Those who focused only on his giraffe physique and aerial threat were oblivious to a tall man's exceptional touch on the deck and his unselfish, unheralded creativity.

A fifth player, Keith Pritchett – whose left foot was sweeter than a dessert trolley – was part of the squad who rose through the divisions and left the club midway through their maiden voyage in the penthouse, but he never played in the top flight for Watford.

If you woke up half the street celebrating Luther's famous goals against Manchester United, if you were there when Ross scored to send the 7-1 miracle against Southampton into extra time, if you let it all hang out behind the goal when Ian's wind-assisted equaliser sailed over Rotherham keeper Ray Mountford from 60 yards, and if you remember Steve's acrobatic defiance at Arsenal as well as Andy Gray's obvious foul in the Cup final, you've never had it so good.

The band of brothers' enduring respect for each other and for the manager who turned them into a formidable, motivated team shines through in their memoirs from a golden age. And if *Rocket Men* serves as four witness statements from an unforgettable era and a timeless tribute to the genius who piloted Watford into unprecedented orbit, hopefully we are left with a definitive chronicle worthy of a brilliant manager and a great man.

There's only one Graham Taylor.

Mike Walters

1

STEVE SHERWOOD

BY MIKE WALTERS

Third Degree

Warbling across the airwaves from Mexico City, 5,500 miles away, David Coleman's commentary crackled through loud and clear as a clan gathered excitably around the TV at home in Selby, the town in Yorkshire's flat Earth society where King Henry I had been born 900 years earlier.

The doyen of BBC's track-and-field coverage was in his pomp as David Hemery surged clear to strike gold for Britain in a world-record time in the men's 400-metres hurdles final at the 1968 Olympic Games, one of only five events where the Union flag was raised highest above central America.

'And David Hemery wins for Britain,' shrieked Coleman. 'In second place it's Hennige [Gerhard Hennige of West Germany], and who cares who came third? It doesn't matter.'

Actually, it did matter who came third. Another British athlete, John Sherwood, took the bronze medal, and among those bursting with pride back home in Selby was his 14-year-old brother, Stephen. Sherwood's achievement may only have warranted a dismissive footnote in Coleman's soundtrack, but when confirmation came through that he had made the podium in a desperately tight finish behind Hemery, the family's celebrations were unrestrained.

'It might not have mattered to David Coleman who came third, but in our house we cared quite a lot,' says Steve

Sherwood, who would go on to forge a notable career in sport for himself. 'I had a fantastic respect for my brother. I looked up to him in every sense. He was an athlete in a time when it wasn't a full-time profession – he was a teacher, and he had to find time to devise his own training routines.

'He used to take me down the local rec, put his hurdles up around the boundary of the cricket pitch and practise his stride patterns. David Hemery won the race, and I'm taking nothing away from his achievement, but he had a scholarship in America which allowed him to prepare on proper surfaces. For my brother to win a bronze medal, when his training facilities were so basic, was incredible. In those days I didn't always look forward to going to school, but the next morning I couldn't wait to get there. I was the brother of an Olympic bronze medallist, and there weren't too many of those knocking around the classroom.

'It was a very close finish and, at first, we thought he might have come fourth, which is the worst place to finish – just outside the medals. Most of the runners crossed the line together behind Hemery, and it was impossible to separate them with the naked eye on a TV screen, so we were jubilant when he was awarded third. I had never seen so many people in Selby when he brought his medal home.'

Sherwood's excitement that summer was not limited to one lap at 8,000ft altitude, however. The following day John's wife, Sheila, was involved in the women's long-jump final in Mexico – and the living room was even more crowded. A platoon of photographers joined the extended family as they tuned in, but in a masterpiece of bad timing the volume control on their TV crashed and an Olympic long-jump competition became a silent movie.

'They were all taking our photo, but we weren't sure if Sheila had won the gold medal because the sound went down,' says

Steve. 'We could see the pictures but there was no commentary, and we were all trying to work out whether she was leading the competition from her facial expressions and body language. As it happens, she won silver, so it was still an amazing feat for a married couple to win bronze and silver at the Olympics. And their success had a big influence on me because I knew how hard they had worked. It taught me the discipline required to reach the top in sport.

'There was pressure on me at school because I was John Sherwood's brother and I was expected to win all the athletics events. I was all right at 100 metres, but I was pretty hopeless at anything over long distance, so I soon found out I wasn't going to be an Olympic athlete like him. When I came to Watford, I was always near the back of Graham Taylor's infamous pre-season cross-country runs through Cassiobury Park, up into Whippendell Woods and back across West Herts golf course – although I wasn't the slowest goalkeeper in the field. Andy Rankin only just managed to finish some of them.'

With Olympic medallists for a brother and sister-in-law, Sherwood's pathway to a career in professional sport was clearly signposted. It was only much later, however, that he realised his father, George, had been a trailblazer for him in football, a discovery augmented by him stumbling across buried treasure on an auction website.

'My dad was a very private man,' says Sherwood. 'He never gave much away, never blew his own trumpet, and I learned more about him after he died than when he was alive. He was a shipbuilder, but later on I discovered he played inside-left for Stockport County, and scored a few goals for them, until the Second World War cut short his career.

'When I was doing a bit of research on him, and typed "George Sherwood Stockport County" into the search engine, the first entry was a signed collectors' card of my dad from the 1938-39 season on eBay. I made sure I stayed ahead of the bidding, paid £14 for it and it's now in a frame on my desk at home.

'He never pushed me into a being a footballer. Coming from Yorkshire and growing up in the era of Fred Trueman, Brian Close, Geoff Boycott and Ray Illingworth, we loved our cricket and I was a decent swing bowler who could bat a bit. I went for trials at Yorkshire, but there were about 100 kids there and I hardly got a look-in. I bowled one over, batted for about six balls and that was it. Dad was not impressed, and said it was a waste of time.'

Yorkshire cricket's loss would be football's gain. The Yellow Brick Road would lead to Watford, where the streets were not paved with gold but the memories would be golden. For a career spanning almost 24 years and 506 senior appearances, Sherwood cost his employers the grand sum of £4,000 in transfer fees – the princely outlay Watford paid Chelsea to bring him to Vicarage Road in 1976. He may not have been the most famous sportsman in his own family but, by any yardstick, he proved astonishingly good value for money.

Content to rely on public transport during his formative years at Stamford Bridge and on loan at Brentford, Sherwood had not even learned to drive by the time he pitched up in Hertfordshire. He eventually passed his test at the age of 25, rolling into training behind the wheel of a modest Datsun Cherry, and nobody followed Graham Taylor's edict that players should live within a ten-mile radius of Vicarage Road to the letter more than Sherwood. Instead of a mock-Tudor mansion or ostentatious palace on a gated private estate, he moved into a terraced house in Harwoods Road, barely a goal-kick from ground.

Like most players in the band of brothers who took Watford on their magic-carpet ride under Taylor, the best years of Sherwood's life were defined by enjoyment and success, not material wealth. 'We didn't earn much, but money wasn't the be-all and end-all,' he says. 'When you're winning like we were, and taking a club to places it had never been before, it really wasn't that important. I can't think of anything more enjoyable than spending 11 years of your life the way we did.'

A Single Man

By all accounts, Mike Keen was an approachable, easy-going and loyal manager, but he suffered the ignominy of leading Watford to relegation into the Fourth Division in 1975 and, briefly, to 92nd in the Football League.

On the night the trapdoor opened, after a harrowing 3-2 home defeat by Walsall, a pitch invasion by hundreds of disaffected patrons was for the attention of chairman Jim Bonser. If the fans were not impressed, they did not lay the blame for the Hornets' lowly plight exclusively at Keen's doorstep. Bonser had kept the purse-strings tighter than the wires in his successor Elton John's grand piano. For the transformation from austerity to prosperity to take root, regime change was the only plausible option.

Keen's last meaningful act in the cockpit at Vicarage Road, before the axe fell, was to hand a young goalkeeper his Watford debut. Steve Sherwood's career had been in danger of gathering dust like a family heirloom in the attic, but in 1977 the first snapshots of an immense contribution to the club's history emerged like the promising glint of buried treasure.

'Mike was a really nice guy,' says Sherwood. 'But if players didn't want to train in the afternoon, or go the extra mile for him, they wouldn't do it. There was nothing wrong with his tactics, but the dressing room was certainly not ruled with an iron fist. It had been the same story when I was at Chelsea – Dave Sexton was the manager, and he was very smart tactically, one of the best, but some of the big-name players like Peter Osgood were as big as him and they knew it. They got away with things in training that would not have got past Graham Taylor.' (Osgood would allegedly hide in the bushes over the back of Epsom Downs, by the racecourse, to avoid Sexton's long-distance runs).

'As a young lad, I had been completely overawed coming down to the bright lights of London. I was totally in awe of Ossie and his mates. I used to clean their boots, sweep the terraces at Stamford Bridge and if they had told me to wipe their backsides for them, I would probably have done that as well. It was quite a hard upbringing for an apprentice in those days – you didn't leave the ground until 5 p.m. and you were back in at half past eight the next morning. It was tough.

'One or two of the players could be a bit nasty – I remember Micky Droy slagging me off during a game at Southampton once – and things like that didn't do much for your confidence. Micky was a great servant to Chelsea, but he was a no-nonsense guy and if something came into his head, he just said it. Although I played a whole season on loan at Brentford, and won the supporters' Player of the Year, I never got an extended run in the side at Chelsea. In five years, I only played 16 games for them.'

Sherwood, as it came to pass, also had to be patient for a first-team opportunity at Watford, making his entrance with Keen's shelf-life at Vicarage Road down to the last grains of sand in the hourglass. On Easter Saturday in 1977, Watford had decorated their only home League setback of the season, against Brentford, with two missed penalties, Dennis Bond and Alan Mayes finding Bees keeper Len Bond an impenetrable barrier in a damaging 1-0 defeat. The 2-2 draw at Stockport 48 hours later on bank-holiday Monday was neither use nor ornament to the Hornets' fading promotion challenge, and Sherwood's debut at Aldershot the following night – yes, three games in four days – proved to be Keen's prelude to the sack.

A 2-1 defeat at the Recreation Ground was enough for the board to pull the plug. Although he presided over a miracle in the final match of his four years in charge, at home to Huddersfield, Keen's fate was already sealed by the time Tony Geidmintis and Mayes were sent off by hapless referee Trevor Spencer, and Keith Mercer's two late goals sealed an improbable win for the Hornets' nine men. If Mercer was the hero, on his home debut it was Sherwood who provided the platform for Keen's last hurrah, sprawling full-length to make crucial saves when the game was goalless.

'I didn't have a lot to do at Aldershot except pick the ball out of the net twice,' recalls the No.1 of his debut. 'The *Watford Observer* gave me four out of ten, which I felt was a bit harsh, and although the players did not know Mike was already on the way out, I guess it was sod's law for him when we pulled that result out of the fire against Huddersfield. You would never have guessed, from the way the lads fought that day, that he was already a goner . . . and we could never have guessed how the next ten years would unfold.'

Chairman Elton John was about to appoint World Cup-winning captain Bobby Moore as Keen's successor when Don Revie – in his last throes as England manager before absconding to the Arabian desert in the summer of 1977 – recommended 32-year-old Taylor, who had been earning rave reviews and breaking records at Lincoln City. Taylor had failed to win any of his first 11 games in charge of the Imps and acknowledged his managerial career was almost stillborn at Sincil Bank. 'I was the youngest manager in the League and the first few games were a disaster: drawn seven, lost four, and the fans had lost patience,' he said. 'They wanted me out – and in a different culture of hire-and-fire, there's no doubt about it:

I could have sunk without trace. A boy of 28 who had a go but failed.'

A last-gasp Terry Branston header against Darlington handed Taylor his first win as a manager at the 12th attempt, and by the time he swept into Vicarage Road – having turned down First Division West Bromwich Albion for an unlikely alliance with a pop star in the fourth tier – GT was hot property. But as Sherwood observes, Taylor did not make wholesale changes to the squad personnel. More than anything, he changed the culture of trepidation, especially away from home, into a school of enterprise.

'In those early days, Graham kept the majority of the squad because we had some decent players,' says Sherwood. 'Where he was a class apart was in recruiting the right characters to knit it all together. Sam Ellis, Dennis Booth and Ian Bolton came in and they were massive influences. I think Sam had forgotten about me, but we actually played together once for Sheffield Wednesday in a testimonial for Jackie Milburn. I was only about 17, and I nearly joined Wednesday after being on their books as a schoolboy, but I hadn't read the script when "Wor" Jackie stepped up to take a penalty in his benefit match – because I saved it. Sam, who was an established centre-half at Wednesday, came up and said, "What did you do that for? You're supposed to let him score!" I was only a young lad, keen to impress, and I just got caught up in the moment.'

One by one, Taylor introduced himself to the players in a series of meetings where the discussion seemed amiable enough, but there was a distinct air of a new headmaster sizing up pupils who had produced disappointing marks in their exams.

'I remember my first chat with Graham in his office – the big chair, little chair trick. He used to have this big office chair behind his desk, and you would be perched on this little seat so he would be looking down on you. He asked you questions that were almost cryptic, and once or twice I remember stumbling and thinking, "This is like a job interview, I didn't answer that one very well." When it was over he told me, "From what I've seen so far, you've got a lot to prove," and, rightly or wrongly, I took that to mean he thought I had potential.

'But it was out on the training pitch where you knew, almost immediately, that you were dealing with someone special. His organisation, attention to detail and repeating the drills until he was satisfied everyone knew their job was a cut above.'

Taylor's forensic eye for every feature of the game followed him to Watford from Sincil Bank. Sherwood and the survivors of Keen's era soon became aware of the tale about Lincoln players practising a single free-kick routine 76 times – seventy-six! – in one session, and instead of being awestruck they marvelled at his fastidious approach. Elton was so enthused by his new manager's approach that he even appeared on the touchline, with a TV crew in hot pursuit, exhorting the crowd to crank up the volume during a 1-0 win against Grimsby.

'He didn't stay there for long,' says Sherwood. 'I think Graham more or less told him, "This is my workplace, yours is the directors' box in the stand." But they were a brilliant double act and obviously they had a great relationship. Funnily enough, I was an Elton John fan before I joined the club. I remember seeing him on *The Old Grey Whistle Test* and I bought his *Empty Sky* album, so when the fans came up with their "Elton John's Taylor-made army" chant, I was a fully paid-up member. Watford was a great fit for me – a dynamic young manager and a pop idol as chairman.

'One game against Reading in the League Cup gave us an early insight into Graham's methods because, from memory, a couple of the goals came from me throwing the ball out to Keith Pritchett at left-back. Afterwards the boss took me to one side and said, "I don't want you throwing the ball out to full-backs – we need it higher up the pitch." His whole philosophy was based on the premise that your opponents can't score if the ball is in their half.'

Sherwood played the first 14 games of the 1977-78 season, of which Watford won 11, and another block of eight matches before Christmas, but ultimately he was forced to job-share with Andy Rankin as the Taylor revolution gathered irresistible momentum. Rankin, the first man to win Watford's Player of the Season gong (and the first to do so twice), was reliable and popular. Kicking was never his forte, and at times he struggled to reach the halfway line, even without a headwind, but his bootleg Bootle humour was a chortling presence in the dressing room and, well into his thirties, he could still make scientists believe that a man could fly. Rankin's last-ditch save at Old Trafford, which left Gordon McQueen on his knees and beating the turf in disbelief, was his crowning glory when the Hornets upset the applecart with a stunning League Cup upset of Manchester United in 1978.

At the same stage of the competition 12 months earlier, Watford had given a fine account of themselves in a narrow 1-0 defeat at West Brom, where they came agonisingly close to forcing a replay as Luther Blissett's late bicycle-kick cannoned off the underside of the bar. That night, it took a thunderous winner from Tony Brown to beat Sherwood and around 4,000 travelling fans serenaded the Hornets with a first airing of the chorus of the blessed: 'We're proud of you.'

Taylor returned the compliment in his programme notes against Crewe the following weekend, and Sherwood observes: 'If we didn't already know we were on to something special, that game at West Brom confirmed it. They were a really good side who were heading for the top six in the First Division, and the way we took the fight to them was so refreshing. Until that point in my career, I had only played for managers who were laid-back characters, but Graham's intensity was like a whirlwind. He kept you on your toes and you never took your place for granted until he pinned the teamsheet on the noticeboard on a Friday lunchtime."

Although his average of conceding a goal-a-game in 22 appearances was far from shabby, especially in a side who returned serve with 43 goals of their own, Sherwood's last appearance of the Fourth Division title-winning campaign was on 10 December in a 2-2 draw at Southport. The season would finish against the same opposition, which turned out to be their last fixture as a Football League club. Forty years ago, wooden-spoonists who finished 92nd in the League were forced to seek re-election to the professional ranks; after cheating the hangman five times, Southport were the last club to fall at the ballot box, being voted out in favour of Wigan Athletic in 1978 and waving goodbye with a 3-2 defeat at Vicarage Road – a match memorable for a moment of slapstick comedy in front of the old Shrodells stand.

On his home debut, young Irish full-back Albert McClenaghan, attempting a throw-in, succeeded only in hurling himself onto the pitch and leaving the ball in touch. Stand-up comedians at the Palladium have been regaled with fewer laughs for one of their best gags. McClenaghan left Watford that summer and little, if anything, is known of his football career thereafter.

More in hope than expectation, on an England cricket tour of New Zealand in 2013 I made preliminary enquiries about McClenaghan's fate. Introducing myself at a pre-Test series reception, in a spirit of sportsmanship and sauvignon blanc I asked Mitchell McClenaghan, the Kiwis' nippy, left-arm swing bowler, if he was by any chance related, distantly or otherwise, to the Hornets' fugitive defender. One blank look,

somewhere between incredulity and disdain, was all it took for
the conversation quickly to switch towards cricket.

* * *

Watford's second consecutive promotion under Graham Taylor
was not the only show in town during the 1978-79 campaign.
For a start, the new electronic scoreboard at the Vicarage
Road end became the popular assembly point for like-minded
younger fans to relocate their choral society from the Rookery.
Visiting Brentford manager and eternal ray of sunshine Bill
Dodgin scorned Watford's new gadget as 'razzmatazz', but
the scoreboard was not the only illuminating feature of a
memorable season.

On the pitch, the Hornets played with the air of a team who
had checked into a hotel and decided the furniture was not to
their taste. Taylor was not going to hang around in the lower
divisions, and as Watford garnished their first four games with
16 goals, they set off on a stupendous League Cup run. Steve
Sherwood was a spectator as Brentford, Newcastle United,
Manchester United and Exeter City fell by the wayside, but he
was called into action after an unfortunate episode that belongs
in one of those anthologies of freakish goalkeeping injuries.

In 1993, when he had moved on to Chelsea, Wimbledon's
1988 FA Cup hero Dave Beasant was ruled out for eight weeks
after dropping a bottle of salad cream on his foot, severing a
tendon in his big toe. Former Manchester United European
Cup winner Alex Stepney allegedly dislocated his jaw bawling
at his defenders during a game at Birmingham in 1975. David
James, once of Watford, pulled a muscle in his back reaching for
the TV remote control and strained a shoulder trying to land a
carp on a fishing expedition. Kasey Keller, the ex-Leicester and
United States keeper, knocked out his front teeth when pulling
his golf clubs from the boot of his car. And Brentford's Chic

Brodie suffered a career-ending injury when he collided with a dog that had run on the pitch, shattering his kneecap.

Sherwood's route back to Watford's first team in 1978 belonged to the same strains of outrageous fortune. 'My first involvement in that League Cup run was the quarter-final against Stoke,' he says. 'Andy Rankin had been performing really well that season until he slipped, taking out the coal at home one night, and broke his collarbone. I shouldn't really say this, but it was a lucky break for me.'

In an age of obsession with the gilded 'big' clubs, it is hard to envisage a goalless draw between Stoke and Watford as the back-page splash in the *Sun*. But as Sherwood kept a clean sheet and the Hornets never yielded an inch at the Potters' old Victoria Ground, the banner headline the following morning read: OH WATFORD, YOU ARE JUST MAGIC. On the basis that comment is free but facts are sacred, it was stunningly accurate newsprint and Watford won the replay 3-1 after extra time to book a two-legged semi-final against reigning champions Nottingham Forest.

Brian Clough's side would go on to win the European Cup that season, but for long periods the Hornets gave as good as they got on a peat bog at the City Ground before going down 3-1 in the first leg. Luther Blissett had headed the Third Division underdogs in front. With Britain in the grip of a harsh winter, the return leg was in doubt and Taylor roped in the players to help Les Simmons, the groundsman, cover the pitch with straw to insulate it against the big freeze.

'One of Graham's ploys, to make sure our minds were on the task, was to get us involved in things like that,' observes Sherwood. 'At the City Ground, the pitch was a swamp – we played really well and losing 3-1 was maybe a bit harsh – but the second game was totally different. The pitch was so firm it didn't help us. Diving around was like lying down in the middle of the road, and it would probably have been better to play the game in normal conditions. It was great to be playing against Peter Shilton, who was probably the best keeper in the world at that time, but from that night on, as far as I was concerned, straw belonged in a barn, not on a football pitch.'

Apart from Brian Pollard's shot smacking the post, Forest rarely looked like surrendering their advantage, and a sterile 0-0 draw left the Hornets to focus on promotion – although their free-scoring procession before Christmas turned into a stumble, and then a white-knuckle ride, as an element of battle fatigue crept in. But everyone loves a happy ending, and Sherwood was back in the side when they took the chequered flag in style.

He says: 'If you could choose a way to win promotion, the night we went up against Hull was just about the perfect script. It was a lovely summer evening, the ground was absolutely packed, and the atmosphere when we ran out before kick-off was incredible. After the World Cup in Argentina the year before, our fans had taken to greeting the team with tickertape – sometimes it was like confetti at a wedding, but that night it was a real blizzard. I don't think Boca Juniors could have done it any better.'

Although the countdown to promotion had made nerves jangle like a charm bracelet, one player was immense on the run-in when the Hornets faltered. Roger Joslyn – who never settled for ballet shoes where hobnail boots were available in his size – may have been one-paced and his shooting from distance often threatened the clock above the Rookery, but his stamina was Olympian and during the severe winter he had chugged through the midfield snow, mudflats, sandbanks and every conceivable surface known to professional footballers.

Whatever Joslyn lacked in finesse, he made up for it with pure 'ticker' – and when a Good Friday meltdown against Colchester, an under-par performance at top-end rivals Swindon,

undeserved defeat at Carlisle and blowing a two-goal lead at home
to Plymouth suddenly left the Hornets' promotion chances in
the balance, 'Jaws' – as the late *Watford Observer* cartoonist Terry
Challis had christened him, with devastating veracity – was a
colossal influence in hauling them over the line.

When the equation boiled down to win or bust against
Hull, it was Joslyn who settled pulse rates among the 26,347
tickertape throwers with an early goal. It wasn't until the last
20 minutes that the party could start in earnest, but by the time
Ian Bolton, Ross Jenkins and Luther Blissett had completed
the procession, Watford had reversed their 4-0 thrashing at
Boothferry Park six months earlier, a freakish result for which
Sherwood now offers a plausible explanation.

Three days before they were humbled on Humberside, the
Hornets had drawn 1-1 at Scarborough in a midweek testimonial
and stayed on the Yorkshire coast afterwards. Mindful of the
approaching League game at Hull, Taylor had counselled
abstinence but, for once, his instruction was ignored. 'It wasn't
a walk in the park against Scarborough – they gave us a hell of
a game and they were trying really hard to turn us over,' says
Watford's keeper that night. 'We weren't supposed to go out
after that game with Scarborough, but everybody crept out and
Graham soon found out about the lads sneaking back into the
hotel at an unwise hour. It was the only time I can remember us
being disciplined for an episode of that nature.

'We were a noisy team – there were some real characters and
chatterboxes – but when Graham came back into the dressing
room after the Hull game, he absolutely slaughtered us: "You're
too loud – you've just lost a game 4-0. Do you not care about
the club?" Nobody dared to move. That was the first time I had
seen Graham crack down hard.'

For Ellis – one of the ringleaders of Watford's unauthorised
night out – the season's nadir would be his last appearance for

the club, although Taylor held him in such high regard that he would enrol him on the coaching staff.

'That was not a great week, to say the least, so it was nice to avenge our worst result on the last day of the season with so much at stake,' says Sherwood. 'It was the perfect happy ending.' As fans danced in the pond at the top of the High Street, celebrating a second successive promotion, and chairman Elton John joined the merrymaking as players took a bow in the directors' box at Vicarage Road, 34-year-old Taylor had clinched his third promotion as a manager.

If Watford had hoped his appointment would have the effect of a whirlwind around the place, they had landed a full-blown tornado. Rarely, if ever, has a single man galvanised a team, a club, a whole town, like GT in his first two seasons with the Hornets. *A Single Man* was the title of Elton's album released during the season, his first for two years. As many fans suspected, when the album was released and the cover shot showed the chairman wearing a club tie, it was a dedication to Taylor's astonishing influence on his boyhood team.

Elton invited the players to provide backing vocals on one of the tracks, 'Georgia', and nearly 40 years later Sherwood cannot decide if it was a privilege or an act of misadventure. 'I don't know what the producers and mixers in the recording studio made of us. There weren't many singing voices in that team who would be headline acts at Glastonbury, and it's probably just as well the track was never released as a single – I'm not sure we would have come across well on *Top of the Pops*. And I've always been glad that we never released a record when we played at Wembley a few years later – when you've got a rock star as chairman, those things are best left to him.'

Turning Point

After leaping halfway up the League ladder in two bounds, Graham Taylor knew there was never the slightest chance of Watford going through the divisions without pausing for breath.

There would have to be a period of consolidation in the Second Division, with upgrades in certain areas of the squad, and sentiment alone could not sustain all the players who had served Watford so well in reaching their plateau. However reluctant the parting of ways, some would have to be discarded. Right-back John Stirk – along with striker Ross Jenkins the only ever-present in all 58 games of the 1978-79 season – was summarily ditched after the Hornets were knocked out of the League Cup at the first hurdle over two legs by Colchester. Stirk became a science teacher after winding down his career. And following the manic Monday night when the Hornets reached the Football League's upper slopes, Steve Sherwood's vocation at Vicarage Road reached the proverbial crossroads. In the next 18 months, he made only five first-team appearances and, under less perceptive management, he could have withered on the vine.

'If you look at the team who went up that night against Hull, it was basically the same one that took a lap of honour at the game with Southend when we were presented with the Fourth Division trophy 12 months earlier,' says Sherwood. 'Steve Harrison arrived early in that season and he was great for a keeper. He used to follow in the opposition's shots – if you could only parry it, or spilled it, he was first on the scene to mop up the rebound and clear the danger. He was a brilliant comedian off the pitch but a great competitor when the whistle blew, almost nasty. Like a dog waiting for the postman. In a way, you felt sorry for Keith Pritchett, who lost his place when Steve arrived, because he had the sweetest left foot and he was a decent penalty-taker. But Keith was not a blood-and-guts defender; he was never going to have a full head of scars like Steve Terry.'

As Taylor strengthened his hand in the Third Division, one transfer had registered more shock waves than a seismograph. Steve Sims joined Watford from Leicester City for £175,000 – then a record fee at that level – in the first instance of the Hornets flexing their muscles financially with a rock-star chairman as their guarantor at the bank. 'If Steve's knee had held up when we reached the top end of our climb, he could have played for England,' says Sherwood. 'He was my roommate and we got on like a house on fire.'

Fighting to gain a foothold in Division Two, Taylor dwarfed his outlay on Sims by bringing in six new players at a total cost of around £700,000 – and one of them was a goalkeeper, Eric Steele. Agile and consistent, Steele's knowledge of his craft became even more evident after his playing career ended. He was hired as specialist goalkeeping coach to Sven-Göran Eriksson at Manchester City, Sir Alex Ferguson at Manchester United and, more recently, by the Football Association as a mentor to England age-group squads.

Sherwood remained in the shadows as Steele played in 58 out of the 59 games following his addition to the Vicarage Road payroll, including the FA Cup run which ended in narrow defeat by Arsenal in the quarter-finals in 1980 and the League Cup miracle against Southampton six months later. But once he was dropped for the quarter-final replay against Coventry, Steele would play in just six of the next 191 competitive games – and only three of them in the League.

Most Watford supporters who were alive on 9 December 1980 will remember it as a lousy day from start to finish. We awoke to news that John Lennon had been murdered in New York overnight, and it ended with a 5-0 thumping defeat at Highfield Road. For Sherwood, however, it marked his resurrection as a first-team goalkeeper.

Watford had been held 2-2 by the Sky Blues at a packed Vicarage Road in the original tie, where new signing Gerry Armstrong's first goal for the Hornets was a real torpedo, and Taylor was concerned that Steele's command of his six-yard area was straying towards timidity. The manager resolved to make a change after a comfortable 2-0 win at home to Notts County, only for Sherwood's comeback to deteriorate rapidly into happy hour on the coconut shy.

'We were a goal down after only two or three minutes, and it didn't get any better. Coventry had this big centre-forward Garry Thompson [who would sign for Watford eight years later] and he just battered us. When I had watched Eric, he hardly ever came out for crosses, and for some reason I decided that I was going to come out and claim everything. I was probably at fault for a couple of the goals that night after Thompson beat me to a couple of crosses, and Graham told me afterwards, "You don't have to come out for everything. Just play your normal game – that's why I've put you back in the team."

'If ever there was a reason for me to be grateful to Graham, that was it. He could have taken the result at face value and said "That's your lot." It would have been easy to single out the goalkeeper after we had been hammered. But when he kept me in the side, it gave me the boost I needed. It made me feel that he actually cared about you, and after that I felt like I needed to repay him – and I felt as if I did repay him in terms of my performances. It's not often that you can say a 5-0 defeat was the best thing that ever happened to you, but that was the start of the best time of my life.'

Watford's progress in 1980-81 was fitful, their FA Cup ambitions ended by undeserved defeat in a replay against Wolves, whose striker Andy Gray would become a familiar nemesis for Sherwood. But when they ended the campaign with three consecutive wins to finish a respectable ninth, it was enough for Taylor to take stock in the summer and declare: 'It's time we made another move.'

One of those three wins to wind down the season was at Notts County, who were forced to put their promotion party on hold by two Luther Blissett goals in driving rain. 'Although it was the end of April, it was probably the coldest I've ever been on the pitch,' says Sherwood. 'It's the only time I've been shivering in the dressing room at half-time, literally shaking with the cold. The rain was like spears.'

The last game was at Wrexham, where Blissett struck another late winner and captain Pat Rice set a template every team has since adopted – by leading the players to applaud hundreds of travelling fans, at least one of whom should have been at home revising for his history mock A-level paper about the Crusades.

When the Hornets returned to north Wales on a Tuesday night early the following season and banked another 1-0 win, it was a throwback to the Seventies as the team travelled home on the fans' special train. For Sherwood, it was also an evening where everything stuck. Wrexham spent the whole second half camped around Watford's box, but the visiting keeper's handling was impeccable and his shot-stopping was invincible.

'I remember Graham pulling me aside after that game and saying, "They were never going to get past you tonight." Nothing does more for a goalkeeper's confidence than clean sheets, and for me it was a neat coincidence that we clinched promotion against Wrexham at the end of that season. The night we went up was the best feeling you can have on a football pitch. I literally got carried away – the fans chaired me off, along with at least two of the other lads. I lost all my gloves to souvenir hunters, and the club made me pay to replace them, but I didn't really care. If you put together the second half of that promotion season, and the first half of our first season in the top flight, that was the best year of my career. There were games where I felt I made a difference – I wasn't necessarily the match-winner, but I made an important contribution – and I can sum up that year in a single word: confidence.

'In all the time I played professional football, I never felt as secure as the games when Pat Rice, Steve Sims, Ian Bolton and Wilf Rostron formed the back four in front of me – and that probably extends to Les Taylor and Kenny Jackett in midfield as well. Week in, week out, you always knew what you were going to get from them. Pat was a fantastic leader of the team as captain, but he was also a big influence on Nigel Callaghan fulfilling his potential – he was always on Cally's case, making sure he stayed switched on.

'And Les was a fantastic competitor. People used to sneer that Watford didn't have a midfield because we supposedly hoofed the ball straight into the final third, so maybe our critics would care to explain how he was our Player of the Season when we went up? I think 1982 was my best year, and I remember it began by knocking Manchester United out of the FA Cup, and Les had a real battle with Bryan Robson. Graham said that was a perfect example of the way we had to take the fight to "big" clubs and not give them too much respect based on reputation. They were just names, and if they are on the floor you don't give them an arm to pull them up.'

If 1982 was the time of his life, Sherwood was there at every landmark game, from the evening Watford went up to the day they went top of the League after five games and the 8-0 annihilation of Sunderland. Watford did not just pull up a few trees that year; they flattened entire forests. He can also reel off games where his performances caught the eye, notably that Cup win against United, a fingertip save to divert Ian Miller's goalbound shot against the bar in a tense win at Blackburn on the run-in to promotion and the North London 'double' as the Hornets beat Tottenham and Arsenal on their own turf three weeks apart. Sherwood's second-half display at Highbury was from the top drawer, as was his full-length sprawl to claw Ian Bowyer's shot around the post at Nottingham Forest, although in that instance his fingertip defiance was in vain as Watford were knocked off the No.1 spot in a 2-0 defeat.

The following week's romp against Sunderland was memorable for all sorts of reasons. It remains Watford's record League victory, Blissett's four goals – his first hat-trick for the club after 19 previous occasions where he had scored twice – earned him an England call-up against West Germany the following month, and for Sherwood a perfect day was rounded off by the birth of his son, Craig, in the hospital next door to Vicarage Road.

Watford's preference for free-scoring, high-tempo, all-out attack did not enjoy the unanimous approval of Fleet Street, where a nucleus of learned scribes seemed to prefer possession and patience as the way forward despite falling attendances. Everyone had an opinion on Graham Taylor's approach, but Sherwood's analysis will resonate far more with fans who lived through it than visiting professors of attrition at Vicarage Road.

When the Hornets had the effrontery to go to White Hart Lane and spoil Glenn Hoddle's comeback from injury – Les Taylor supplying the late goal for a 1-0 win – they forced 19 corners. Whether they made full use of them is another matter, but that statistic spoke volumes for the endeavour of an away side refusing to bow and curtsey on a big club's stage.

'For what it's worth, I felt Graham's philosophy was right in a lot of ways. I don't think it's the complete package, but it was based on scoring goals – and in an entertainment industry, I don't see how that can be a drawback. Other teams were trying to play in a continental fashion, with keepers throwing the ball out to the full-backs, and we didn't give them a moment's peace. Ross, Luther and Gerry Armstrong were fit lads, and they would win the ball back for us high up the pitch. People talk these days about pressing as if it is a new tactic or someone had reinvented the wheel, but it was a real cornerstone of Graham Taylor's philosophy. Luther's goalscoring record speaks for itself, but he was just as important to us when we didn't have the ball. Defenders who wanted to stroll around and stroke passes in the name of culture simply weren't afforded the time or space.

'If we had tried to play in a "sophisticated" manner, as Graham used to call it, we wouldn't have even finished halfway up the table, but we were fearless. At home, when we ran out I always felt so confident that we weren't just going to beat the other lot – we were going to marmalise them, and we often carried that mentality into away games as well. When we went to Arsenal and won 4-2, it could have been about 10 each. That was probably my best game in the season when we finished runners-up.'

Laced with poison or not, the giddy narrative of Watford's rise to prominence, briefly hitting the First Division summit in September 1982 and finishing their debut season in the top flight as runners-up to Liverpool, became one of English football's biggest feel-good stories. Less well-known, as the Hornets took complacent aristocrats by storm, is that Sherwood was close to an England call-up in the early days of Bobby Robson's reign as the national team's manager. That he never broke into the international set-up is no surprise; it was always going to be a tall order to dislodge Peter Shilton and Ray Clemence from the pecking order, but it was a measure of Sherwood's consistency that he was in the frame.

'I was told my name was on a list, which was a real boost at a time when England were almost spoilt for choice,' he says. By the early 1980s, Shilton may just have peaked in an international career spanning 20 years, but he went on to play in three World Cup tournaments. And in Sherwood's decade at Watford, opportunities for other keepers to oust the nation's most-capped player were few and far between. Joe Corrigan, Gary Bailey and Nigel Spink all got a look-in, while Clemence was coming to the end of his 61-cap career and the promising Chris Woods made his Three Lions debut in 1985, but none seriously threatened to unseat Shilton.

It was a major achievement that Sherwood's form, in the heady days when Watford were reaching for the sky, even put him in contention to play for England. Whatever lay around the corner amid the pomp and pageantry when he did make it to Wembley on club business, that was the true measure of his ability and his contribution to the Hornets' rise from obscurity.

Europe

Saturday 14 May 1983 – the day Watford qualified for Europe – was, statistically at least, the high-water mark in the club's history.

A season blessed with more highlights than a hair salon came to a sunny conclusion with a 2-1 win at Vicarage Road over runaway champions Liverpool. There are still people who believe the biggest cheer, after the final whistle, greeted news of the old enemy's escape from the jaws of relegation with a last-gasp winner at Manchester City, which sent a man in a beige suit cavorting across the pitch at Maine Road. Really? How about the bulletin informing us of Manchester United succumbing late at Meadow Lane, where Notts County's 3-2 win meant Watford had leapfrogged the FA Cup finalists to finish as runners-up in the League? The second-best team in the country. No beige at the Vic – just Golden Boys.

Steve Sherwood remembers the moment vividly: 'After we beat Liverpool, their keeper Bruce Grobbelaar came into our dressing room and said, "Well done – for you to finish second is a better achievement than us winning the title," and I think he meant it. He said they didn't lay down and let us beat them because it was Bob Paisley's last game as manager before he retired. That was big of him to be so complimentary. These days you would hear talk of them being "on the beach" or other excuses, but Liverpool pushed us all the way that afternoon.'

Ultimately, the Hornets were only cleared to get their passports stamped on a European tour in the UEFA Cup by an extraordinary miss, spooned over the top from three yards out, by Kenny Dalglish as they clung on grimly to their slender lead. Martin Patching, making a storybook return from major knee surgery, and Luther Blissett's 30th goal of the season for club and country had put Watford in the driving seat, but Craig Johnston halved the Kop's deficit and, for all the euphoria that greeted the historic alignment of results, there was an outpouring of relief before the happy-ever-after for most of the 27,073 crowd.

'Dalglish and Ian Rush was the best partnership I faced in my career,' recalls Sherwood. 'Dalglish was so clever because he could cut you open with one weighted pass nobody else could play, and Rush was absolutely lethal, especially over the first ten yards. They took us apart at Anfield that season. It would have been a privilege to watch if it hadn't been so impossible to stop them.'

Watford in Europe . . . like the holiday of a lifetime, you wish it could have gone on for longer but it was fabulous while it lasted. Three-time European Cup winner Paisley's wise words sprang readily to mind: 'In Europe you moan about the travel, the hotels, the food and the referees, but once you are out . . . God, you don't half miss it.'

Of course, Fleet Street's critics of their so-called long-ball football reckoned they would be eliminated from the UEFA

Cup before the cross-Channel ferry from Dover had docked in Calais. First stop on the Hornets' European tour was Kaiserslautern, the formidable Germans whose ranks included Hans-Peter Briegel, a rugged defender, Dolph Lundgren lookalike, and winner of 72 international caps for West Germany. The perceived wisdom was that Watford would need to return from Kaiserslautern's Betzenberg fortress, at the summit of a steep sandstone hill, with only a minimal deficit to overturn in the second leg at Vicarage Road. They went down 3-1, but the margin of defeat was slightly harsh and Jimmy Gilligan's away goal was a useful bargaining chip as well as a unique footnote in the club's history. Establishment purists, conveniently overlooking a prodigious injury list, predictably sneered that Watford had been found out. In truth, they had fallen foul of the oldest trick in the book: sleep deprivation.

'Before the game in Kaiserslautern, the plan was to get there early, have a meal and grab a couple of hours' sleep in the hotel,' says Sherwood. 'But when we got to the hotel, there were loads of German fans hanging around outside, blowing whistles and ringing bells constantly. They must have found out where we were staying and, needless to say, we didn't get much sleep. But it wound us up and made us show them what we were about. We were right in the game at 2-1 down when the big lad up front [Torbjörn Nilsson, a Swedish international who played under former England coach Sven-Göran Eriksson at IFK Gothenburg] scored a late third. I swear he mishit it – he was trying to volley it into the roof of the net and he toe-poked it almost underneath me. It was a bit of a sickener; we didn't deserve that.'

Watford's injury crisis had not abated by the time Kaiserslautern breezed into Hertfordshire for the return, and their mission to overturn the two-goal shortfall was not helped by a home defeat against Tottenham on the preceding weekend. That was the game in which any blame for Glenn Hoddle's audacious chip over Sherwood, drifting under the angle of bar and far post, was somehow laid at the door of the Hornets' stranded keeper. Whether or not Hoddle's goal was an act of intentional genius or an exquisite pitching wedge, 'standing up' a cross for strikers to devour at the far post, it was hardly Sherwood's fault.

But manager Graham Taylor had sensed an air of complacency about the Germans, who evidently believed the tie was already won. After asking groundsman Les Simmons to leave a gate ajar at the top of Occupation Road, Taylor sneaked in to watch Kaiserslautern go through their paces the night before the second leg – not an act of industrial espionage to glean tactical information, but a covert operation to gauge the opposition's mood. He was struck by the 'frivolous' nature of their drills and hotch-potch dress code of jeans, trainers and casual clothing.

'They didn't know what hit them,' says Sherwood. 'The atmosphere in the ground that night was fantastic – I remember running on the pitch through a cordon of flags and one of the flags wrapped right round me. The boss wanted to create a more "continental" environment, to set the game apart from normal home fixtures, and his wish was granted.'

Within ten minutes, Kaiserslautern's lead had been wiped out. Ian Richardson, on his debut, gave Watford the perfect start and then Charlie Palmer's cross bounced over the line after an inadvertent ricochet off Werner Melzer. Richardson, stretching to meet Richard Jobson's cross, somehow managed to funnel an improvised finish over visiting keeper Armin Reichel to put the Hornets ahead on aggregate with his second goal of the night 11 minutes after the break, leaving Watford more than half an hour to negotiate.

They lived on their nerves, Reiner Geye's close-range volley miraculously deflected over the bar by a combination of Steve

Terry's knee and Sherwood's hand. 'I'm still not sure how we smuggled that one over the top,' admits the keeper with a rueful smile. 'But I know we didn't want it to go to extra time and I know that, over the two legs, we deserved to go through.'

When Levski Spartak of Sofia, packed with Bulgarian internationals, held Watford to a 1-1 draw at Vicarage Road in the first leg of round two, it looked as if the Hornets' European tour would be short-lived. But when Watford ventured behind the Iron Curtain for the return, they produced arguably the greatest single result in the club's history. The story of their Bulgarian adventure was told through my nostalgic recollections in *Tales From The Vicarage* volume 2, but it was a magnificent performance not least because, in many cases, the players had known only reserve-team intensity in the Football Combination.

Nigel Callaghan followed up his spectacular equaliser by delivering an inch-perfect corner to the near post in extra time for Steve Sims to apply a telling flick and Wilf Rostron soared to head the Hornets in front. Richardson snatched another to make it 3-1 on the night, and 55,000 screeching Bulgarians resorted to lighting bonfires on the terraces of the sprawling Vasil Levski stadium, either in protest or surrender.

'Cally was certainly the best crosser of a ball I've ever seen,' says Sherwood. 'When he first came to the club, Graham Taylor asked me what I didn't like as a goalkeeper, what parts of the job I found the most difficult or disconcerting, and one of things I mentioned was crosses whipped in with pace and a bit of shape because they only needed the slightest touch and you were beaten. You don't know whether to follow the trajectory of the cross or wait – to see if a striker gets a flick – and hope your reflexes are in good nick. Sofia was one of Cally's best games for Watford. He was superb that night – in fact, the whole team was fantastic. They really came out of the blocks at us, and the noise from the crowd was incredible: It was like 50,000 whistling kettles going off at once.'

A naïve performance at home against Sparta Prague in the third round – when Watford trailed 2-0 at the interval and went to Czechoslovakia 3-2 down from the first leg – proved too great a handicap. On a rutted, frozen pitch unfit for Torvill and Dean, never mind professional football, the Hornets were caned 4-0 in the second leg and their only European campaign to date met a frozen end. It was like *Ice Station Zebra*, only colder.

'We were well beaten, but the conditions were so farcical it didn't take any of the gloss off what we had achieved in the earlier rounds,' claims Sherwood. 'When we trained on the pitch the night before the game, it was firming up but it was playable – but on the day there was about three inches of snow. They brushed most of it off, but it looked like an athletics track with white pinstripes running straight down the pitch. Our lads couldn't stay on their feet.

'The team that went out of Europe bore very little relation to the one that qualified because we had so many injuries and some of the new signings weren't eligible to play in the UEFA Cup. Things weren't quite the same.'

Fifty Shades of Gray

It was a foul. Of course it was a foul. A blatant, barging, bovine foul. It probably signalled the beginning of the end for Steve Sherwood as Watford's first-choice goalkeeper and, to myopic football-watchers who had never seen him play before, it became his legacy.

Andy Gray's mid-air, bull-in-a-china-shop challenge on Sherwood in the 1984 FA Cup final should have been disallowed by referee John Hunting. When he allowed it to stand, it killed the game as a contest. It also marked the football equivalent of the Glorious Twelfth, open season for every judge and jury to pour scorn on Sherwood as a weak link, an alleged liability on crosses and an expedient scapegoat. Those who had followed his career more attentively, beyond a single incident beamed around the world, knew differently.

Of the four legends featured in this volume, only one was there through every promotion, the raiding parties in Europe and the Cup final, without any interruptions. Ross Jenkins prepared for his assault on the League's upper slopes with a sojourn on loan across the big pond at Washington Diplomats; Luther Blissett spent a year at AC Milan as Watford's first million-pound export before his repatriation 12 months later; and Ian Bolton's raking passes, 'explosion' free-kicks and defensive mobility decorated all four divisions before he joined Brentford midway through the 1983-84 season.

But Steve Sherwood was there when Graham Taylor walked through the door as manager in 1977, and he remained faithful to the end of the messiah's first incarnation at Vicarage Road – not always in the first team, not always appreciated and, due to the quality of the man who took his place, probably not in many Watford supporters' all-time fantasy XI picks. Yet when GT was sprinkling stardust in industrial quantities during three consecutive seasons when he turned promotion, Europe and Wembley from our distant horizons into our dreams come true, Sherwood missed only three League games. He was as essential to the plot as the wheels on a plane – often taken for granted, but you wouldn't half miss them if they were not there.

Sherwood was not the first goalkeeper to leave the FA Cup-final stage with regrets. As far back as 1927, when Cardiff City beat Arsenal, Hughie Ferguson's winning goal was fumbled over the line by Gunners keeper Dan Lewis, who blamed the shot squirming from his grasp on the sheen of new wool on his previously unworn jersey. Since then, out of superstition or tradition, Arsenal have washed their goalkeeper's jersey before every match. And Gary Sprake was forever haunted by his mistake in the 1970 final, when the Wembley pitch had been reduced to a ploughed field by the Horse of the Year Show, as he dived over the top of Peter Houseman's shot in the 2-2 draw between Leeds and Chelsea.

But Gray's collision with Sherwood – the most charitable way of expressing the pair's brief encounter – was like no other at Wembley since Bolton's Nat Lofthouse had barged into Manchester United keeper Harry Gregg in the 1958 final, depositing him over the line with the ball. Lofthouse's challenge, like Gray's, was deemed legitimate and the goal was allowed to stand. Destiny had foretold that United would lift the Cup just three months after the Munich disaster. When Bolton returned home with the famous old pot, their coach was stoned by United supporters as it drove through Kearsley, on Manchester's northern fringes, on the journey from Piccadilly station. Twenty-six years later, Watford fans accepted Everton's 2-0 win more graciously, although that moment in time did nothing for Sherwood's reputation.

* * *

Let's be honest – the journey to Wembley was a lot of fun. During an era of hooligan excess, we swayed down English football's most celebrated promenade, yellow and red mingling happily with blue and white, and it became known as the 'friendly final' – yet another tribute, as if any more were required, to the inclusive and sociable manner Taylor had cultivated among his flock. And if the retreat was bathed in disappointment and anti-climax, the adventures Watford survived on the road to their first major final were unforgettable.

When the third-round draw was made, even the most brazenly optimistic Hornets fans would have invested little disposable income on the Yellow Brick Road leading to Wembley. A short trip to Kenilworth Road was just about the most thankless assignment the tombola of balls in the velvet bag could have handed Taylor.

In seven League meetings with the old enemy, GT had mustered only a single point to show for his team's labours. Four previous defeats at a horrid ground Father Time forgot had left little doubt that fortune smiled more at Eric Morecambe's best one-liners than at Elton John's greatest hits – and fortune was a Hatter, yet again, as two deflected goals left Watford 2-0 down inside 20 minutes. Not before time, fate was kinder to the Hornets as John Barnes and a Mo Johnston penalty levelled it up before the break, and Watford came closest to winning the tie at the first time of asking when Nigel Callaghan skimmed the bar so late his shot only just beat the opening bars to 'Out Of The Blue', the brisk march which signals BBC Radio's *Sports Report* at the top of the hour.

The replay at Vicarage Road three days later was a classic, arguably the best derby game – win or lose – against the heretics in half a century or more. 'Goalkeepers don't usually recall games where there were seven goals with much fondness, but that replay was an absolute belter,' says Sherwood. 'In the end, it all boiled down to willpower.'

This time, it was the Hornets who raced into a two-goal lead thanks to Callaghan's audacious chip and George Reilly, and when Barnes made it 3-1 early in the second half a fourth-round trip to Charlton appeared to be in the bag. But two Paul Walsh goals forced the extra half-hour, and it was the visitors who blinked first, Johnston's header proving decisive on a night of spellbinding tension.

'All the times they had beaten us in the League over the previous four or five years,' muses Sherwood. 'I wonder if they would have traded those wins for the FA Cup tie, knowing where it took us. We didn't have it all our own way at Charlton, and for 20 minutes we were a bit shaky in the fifth round against Brighton. If anything, it was the games where we were expected to win comfortably that we struggled more, but we stood up tall in the quarter-final at Birmingham. That was the acid test, and we came through it.'

Watford had never won at St Andrew's when they came up against the Bluenoses – a combustible, rugged team in their manager Ron Saunders' own image and featuring a certain Tony Coton in goal. With Noel Blake, Mick Harford and Pat van den Hauwe also in their line-up, Birmingham could have formed a world-class five-a-side squad of bouncers – but fortunately the Hornets were trying to reach the FA Cup semi-finals for only the second time in their history, not gain entry to a nightclub.

When Watford had slumped to a supine 2-0 defeat at Birmingham early in the season, there were only 11,931 fans in attendance; this time, there were nearly four times as many punters and St Andrew's was a heaving cauldron. Not for the first time in the 1983-84 season, Sherwood made his presence felt at both ends of the pitch.

Barnes – zig-zagging between hapless Blues full-back Mark McCarrick and Robert Hopkins in one of those delicious see-you-later manoeuvres which belonged more on a dance floor than the left wing – fired the Hornets in front with a glorious, dipping, bending shot that arched over Coton in a moment of irresistible quality. The ball had sat up for Barnes off a benign bobble on the surface, leading to Saunders' absurd post-match claim that he had 'mishit' his shot. Yes, Ron – he mishit it right into the top corner.

Sherwood has often wondered if, in the stats-obsessed world of modern football, he would have been credited with an assist. After all, Barnes had picked up the ball fewer than 30 yards from goal after the Watford keeper's enormous clearance – which would have pitched inside Birmingham's 18-yard area without Blake heading it half-clear, postponing the danger but not extinguishing it.

'If I wasn't making saves, Graham told me I was an important part of our attacking play,' says Sherwood. 'Earlier that season, I had scored when we won 2-1 at Coventry. I wasn't going for goal as such, but I had the wind behind me and I knew that a decent connection would put the ball in the opposition box. Their keeper, Raddy Avramovic, came too far off his line to collect it. I think Cally might have distracted him and it went in on the first or second bounce. I was pleased with that.

'At Birmingham in the Cup, where you could feel the atmosphere was simmering, I like to think I played my part. We dominated the first half by getting at them in the final third of the pitch, and I was encouraged to get the ball down there as much as possible to put them under pressure. We had our backs to the wall for much of the second half, and it was a bit hairy for a while after they equalised, but I played all right and we finished them off with a couple of late goals.'

Harford, who had forced Steve Terry to put through his own goal for Birmingham's equaliser, later found Sherwood perfectly positioned to catch his textbook chest-trap and volley with the dexterity of a slip fielder in a Test match. 'He was a good player, Harford. And he was the only opponent who ever hurt me,' says Sherwood. 'For some reason, Michael Robinson had headbutted me at Brighton the previous season, and left me with blood trickling into my eye, but that didn't hurt – not as much as the night when Harford headed me into the post. I think I had caught him when I came to punch a corner and he clattered me. That was the only time in my career I was physically hurt by a forward.'

Les Taylor's rising left-foot shot, which arrowed under the angle of Coton's right-hand post and crossbar, and a coup de grâce applied by the ever-elusive Barnes at the far post from one of Watford's expertly drilled set-piece routines – Callaghan's long throw was the launch pad for this one – finally drew the sting from Birmingham's rally. For some of Watford's 10,000 travelling fans, the journey home from Small Heath was more scenic than expected: somehow I found myself kettled by police and frogmarched back towards New Street station in a cordon of local neanderthals who would not have taken kindly to their sizeable band of brigands being infiltrated.

Once we were all home, with or without a full contingent of glazing in our transport, attention turned inevitably to the semi-final draw, where Everton, Southampton and Watford were all after the same catch: Third Division strugglers Plymouth Argyle or relegation-bound Second Division Derby County, who would replay at Home Park. No disrespect to either club, but it was a one-trick menu. When you walk into Nandos, you want chicken; when you go for lunch at Pizza Express, you want pizza; and when you are in the FA Cup semi-final draw with Everton, Southampton and Plymouth or Derby, you want Plymouth. On the Monday after their resolute performance in the last eight at St Andrew's, Taylor gave his players the morning off so they could listen to the draw at lunchtime and get their heads around the task awaiting them, one step from Wembley.

'I remember being in the car on the way to training, and stopping in a lay-by when the draw was being made, and of course we got the draw we wanted,' says Sherwood. 'But looking back, I was more nervous for that game against Plymouth than I was for the Cup final. I've only watched it back a few times, and it still makes me nervous. But as well as they played, Plymouth didn't really open us up until the last minute. We had a spell, after George Reilly's goal, where we could have put the game to bed, so we weren't lucky to win – but we were relieved it didn't go to extra time.'

Watford fans in the yellow half of the sprawling Holte end at Villa Park were heart-in-mouth when Argyle's Kevin Hodges, inside the box, sliced his shot inches wide of Sherwood's post as the stopwatch ticked round to Wembley o'clock. When it skidded wide, and Plymouth centre-half Lindsay Smith sank to his knees, indicating how close it was with his thumb and forefinger, the die was cast: seven years after taking over a club which didn't know whether they wanted to play football or unleash hounds around a dog track, Graham Taylor's reign was heading for consecration at the cathedral of English football.

'The journey home was the best of them all. Coming back on that coach, I've never been as drunk as that in my life,' says Sherwood. 'You can't explain how good the feeling was. We all had to be picked up and poured into taxis at the other end. We had not made any assumptions, we didn't take any champagne up to Villa Park on the coach with us. But on the return trip, crates of beer started to appear and they just kept coming. If you look at the side we put out in the semi-final and at Wembley, it wasn't the greatest Watford team of all – it must have been the youngest back four in FA Cup-final history – but nobody can ever take that achievement away from them. And when we had something to celebrate, we were a thirsty bunch.'

Seven days after their triumphant retreat, Watford made a less exultant encore at Villa Park, losing 2-1 in the League with a side more patched up than a patchwork quilt. Wilf Rostron – hardly the most towering presence at the back in terms of height – had played as an emergency centre-half in a goalless draw with Manchester United in between the trips to Spaghetti Junction, but for the Hornets captain, the countdown to Wembley would prove to be booby-trapped and full of heartbreak.

Even now, more than 30 years on, the sense of injustice that Rostron missed out on the biggest day of his sporting life burns more fiercely than the blast furnace at a steelworks. The red card, received on enemy territory at Kenilworth Road, which robbed him of leading out Watford in the FA Cup final was a travesty in its own right; that he was deprived of the privilege after contributing so much to Taylor's magic-carpet ride was truly sickening.

Rostron's only crime, as the recipient of a poor challenge by Luton defender Paul Elliott – whose own career would later be curtailed by a dreadful tackle – was to remonstrate with the offender. There has never been a shred of evidence to suggest he threw a punch or retaliated with violence in any way, but referee Roger Milford saw fit to expel both players. Milford's Shirley Temple coiffure and wristbands gave the impression that when he looked in the bathroom mirror, he liked what he saw.

Handing in the teamsheets before kick-off, Taylor had told him: 'You won't get any trouble out of my players today – they have got the FA Cup final in three weeks.' The Watford manager realised the ramifications of Milford's distorted application of the laws immediately. By his own admission, he was lucky to escape serious disciplinary action himself after grabbing Milford by the throat in the tunnel afterwards. Taylor took his wife, Rita, out to watch a Shakespeare play later that night but hated every minute of it – nothing to do with the bard or the acting but because the inequity of Rostron's sending-off was so unfair. By the time Milford awarded Liverpool a hugely contentious penalty two years later, with Watford leading 1-0 four minutes from the end of an FA Cup quarter-final replay, he had become a seasoned highwayman in the eyes of Watford supporters.

'To lose Wilf was an enormous setback,' admits Sherwood. 'He was so consistent, and such an unflappable character. To this day, I don't know what he did to deserve being sent off

– but I know a once-in-a-lifetime opportunity was taken away from him. And of course it took the gloss off beating Luton on their ground for the first time in about 20 years. I knew something was up when I got back in the dressing room. I think I was one of the last ones off the pitch that day, and when you've beaten your local rivals you expect the lads to be full of it – but the euphoria was very muted, if there was any at all.'

In the two previous seasons, Queen's Park Rangers defender Glenn Roeder had missed his side's replay against Tottenham after falling foul of the FA's disciplinary rulebook, and in 1983 Brighton's Steve Foster – later to surface on the heathen side of the Hertfordshire/Bedfordshire border – was ineligible to face Manchester United in the final, only to make the showpiece after all when the Seagulls forced a replay after a 2-2 draw. Foster was probably the only Brighton player who was not completely crestfallen when Gordon Smith's yawning, last-gasp chance to cause a major upset was smothered by United keeper Gary Bailey, the incident enshrined by the late Peter Jones' commentary on BBC Radio: 'And Smith must score . . . and he hasn't scored, Bailey has saved it.'

But where Roeder and Foster both enjoyed the full privileges of FA Cup-final pomp and circumstance, in either the original game or its sequel, there was no reprieve for Rostron. When Milford expressed sympathy for the inconsolable Watford full-back, Taylor dismissed his retrospective remorse as 'sanctimonious claptrap'.

* * *

Apart from senior statesman Pat Rice, who took a curtain call against his former club Arsenal a week before the FA Cup final with right-back David Bardsley racing against the clock to be fit after straining knee ligaments in training, the countdown to Wembley was unchartered territory for Watford's players.

Graham Taylor named his team during the week, in an effort to settle a few nerves among his chosen XI, and the squad spent the week at the Hilton hotel on the A41 at Aldenham, which was the customary bolthole for new signings and players awaiting the keys to their own property. Steve Sherwood found the whole experience fraught with excitement but vaguely unsettling.

'You were taken out of your comfort zone, away from your families,' he says. 'You could feel there was something special going on, but we trained in a field – that's the only way I can describe it – because our normal training ground at Stanmore was out of commission.'

Mercifully, Taylor had declined the opportunity for Watford to record a Cup-final pop song, as was the tradition among many teams heading for Wembley. Where Spurs had piled into the recording studio with Chas and Dave, the Hornets chose not to steal their own chairman's thunder. Elton John was about to release his single 'Sad Songs (Say So Much)' from his forthcoming album *Breaking Hearts*, and the nation was spared a musical gimmick from his employees.

When the big day dawned, Michael Barrymore had been assigned to provide pre-match 'entertainment' for the Hornets. Barrymore's clowning around was harmless enough at first, but his 'tribute' to John Barnes – which was straight from the archives of outdated programmes like *The Black and White Minstrel Show* – would never make it past twenty-first-century arbiters of taste now. 'In fairness, he was funny at breakfast,' says Sherwood. 'He was larking around and the boys seemed relaxed enough but, looking back, he probably stayed on a bit too long. He became a distraction we didn't need.'

The ten-mile journey to Wembley, tracked overhead by a TV news crew's helicopter, passed without incident, but after inspecting the pitch in their Cup-final suits, Sherwood felt Watford's warm-up was impeded . . . by the marching band. Although pre-match routines in 1984 were not assault courses of bibs, cones, hopscotch and shooting wildly into the crowd as they are today, goalkeepers liked to feel the grass beneath their feet and the ball between their hands before kick-off.

Sherwood believes he was denied the space to go through his paces by men in bearskin hats and tunics playing the trombone, saying: 'I don't know if they were camped in our half of the pitch, but we seemed to be kept waiting forever by the band. By the time there was enough room to catch a few crosses, everyone was getting ready for "Abide With Me" and then kick-off. It was bizarre. You like to have a warm-up, you like to have a dive around on the turf, and I remember being bloody annoyed by the band because you want to be properly prepared for the biggest game of your life. But I'll never forget that walk up the tunnel and emerging into the sunlight. At first, all we could see was blue and white, because Everton fans were allocated the far end of Wembley, but then you turned round and saw all those yellow, black and red flags behind us. It was an incredible sight.

'The worst part was feeling we let all those people down by losing. We had been used to success, and giving the fans what they wanted, and the reception they gave us on the lap of honour, and in the town the following morning, was remarkable. It's as if they forgave us on the final whistle. And of course Elton's tears in the Royal Box, because he was so moved by "Abide With Me", became one of the FA Cup final's defining images.'

For around 35,000 Watford supporters, 19 May 1984 was a splendid day out ruined only by an hour of football and one lousy decision. The Hornets were the better side for at least the first quarter of the match, John Barnes spurning two major opportunities and Les Taylor, taking over as captain for the suspended Rostron, seeing his low shot deflected inches wide.

But Everton seized control seven minutes before the break when Graeme Sharp's instinctive finish, from a fortuitous ricochet, left Sherwood stranded. And then, six minutes into the second period, Leicester referee Hunting's see-no-evil interpretation of a mid-air body-check killed a promising game stone-dead as a contest.

Trevor Steven had been giving Neil Price, Rostron's deputy at left-back, a guided tour of Everton's right flank when he whipped a cross beyond the far post, the ball teasing Sherwood with its flight path, and the Watford keeper, back-pedalling furiously, just about managed to get both hands on it while still airborne. But Andy Gray, charging in to meet the cross, had bulldozed Steve Terry out of the way – probably a foul in its own right – and he made no contact with the ball. Gray effectively headed the back of Sherwood's left arm, sending the ball bouncing tamely over the line, and Hunting saw fit to let the goal stand.

'I've never had a problem with Andy Gray,' says Sherwood. 'He was only doing his job, like a good centre-forward should. It's the referee who shouldn't have been able to sleep at night. Even though we were 1-0 down at half-time, we had been the better team. But that second goal killed us off. After that, it was a non-event. Maybe 60 years ago, when centre-forwards were allowed to batter goalkeepers, it might have been allowed. But I will never accept it was a goal when Gray didn't even touch the ball – all he did was barge one defender out of the way and knock it out of my grasp by nutting my arm. People say I never had the cross fully under my control, but it's a bit difficult to have it under control when you are being clattered in mid-air.

'Even after watching it again on TV, Mr Hunting still claimed he made the right decision, but most people knew it was a foul. There was at least one camera angle which showed, clear as day, that I've got both feet off the ground, two hands on the ball

and he's headed my forearm . . . but what can you do? The fans
were brilliant about it, but the next day I got slaughtered in the
papers. Absolutely crucified. All my family had come down,
and they didn't know where to look when I was getting called
"Stevie Blunder" in the headlines and I didn't really deserve it.
Sometimes you need a thick skin to be a goalkeeper, but you
would have needed an elephant's hide not to be hurt by some
of the criticism I got for being fouled. It was a real low point
in my career.'

From the moment Gray bundled in his goal, Watford's race
was run. They went through the motions of a fightback, and
24-goal leading scorer Mo Johnston had a late goal disallowed
for offside, but Everton could lean on vast experience where
the Hornets' back four, from right to left, were aged 19, 21, 18
and 20, while wingers Barnes and Nigel Callaghan were 20 and
21, and midfielder Kenny Jackett was 22.

'Individually, each member of that back four was worth his
weight in gold,' observes Sherwood. 'David Bardsley was so
quick he could almost fly, Steve Terry was brave, Lee Sinnott's
long throws were incredible and although Neil Price didn't
play that many games for Watford, nearly all of them were
big occasions. But as a unit, they didn't quite provide as much
security as Rice, Sims, Bolton and Rostron. That's no criticism
of their ability – they were just very young and they hadn't
played together very often.'

For Sherwood, who didn't do a lot wrong at Wembley, a
close encounter with fifty shades of Andy Gray probably
hastened the end for him as Watford's first-choice keeper. There
were no clean sheets in the first eight games of the following
season (and only one for the Hornets' opponents, to be fair),
and he was powerless to stop the creeping insinuations that his
confidence had been damaged by his Cup-final adventure.

By the time Watford and Everton met again, in a remarkable nine-goal romp at Vicarage Road four months later, manager Graham Taylor had signed Tony Coton from Birmingham for £300,000. Conceding five goals on his debut at home proved to be a bogus foretaste of Coton's virtues, but for Sherwood there would be only 18 more appearances in Watford's No.1 jersey over the next three years before his time was up.

He would bump into Andy Gray at a social function a couple of years after the Cup final and later he told the *Daily Mail*: 'Andy was with the comedian Freddie Starr, who was a mad Everton fan, and Freddie shouted, "Hello, here comes Dracula – doesn't like crosses." I had to laugh. I never had any qualms with Andy Gray. It's the referee I hate.'

Mud sticks, and the careless whisper that Sherwood was vulnerable on crosses was as cloying as it was a travesty. Down the years, you could probably count on the fingers of one hand the number of crosses Sherwood had dropped or treated like a bar of soap in the shower. 'If I'm honest, shot-stopping was my forte,' he says. 'I could have been a bit more dominant, but I didn't have the loudest of voices for bawling out defenders. Vocally, I simply wasn't strong enough to play the barking sergeant major and that's something I could have done better, but I always thought I was decent at dealing with crosses because I didn't drop many.'

Gray's goal against Watford may have been legitimate in Nat Lofthouse's era, but it remains one of the most contentious goals scored at Wembley since a linesman from Azerbaijan signalled that Geoff Hurst's shot against the underside of the bar had crossed the line at the 1966 World Cup final, and Sherwood is still wheeled out occasionally to relive it.

'A few years back, Andy was presenting a show on TV and he didn't know I'd been lined up as a guest when his co-host said to him, "We've got someone on the line here and he's not very

happy with you about something that happened a long time ago."
Quick as a flash, Andy replied, "Oh God, it's not Steve Sherwood
is it? I'm sick of people telling me it was a foul," so I told him
again. "But it was a foul!" He knows that I've got no problem
with Andy Gray – my gripe has always been with the referee. At
the end of the day, if I was a manager, I would want a player like
him in my team because I grew up in an age when the first thing
a centre-forward did was to hit the goalkeeper.'

Finger of Fate

Graham Taylor's wife Rita chose Watford's red goalkeeper's
jersey, as worn by Steve Sherwood in the FA Cup final.

When kit suppliers Umbro sent through a new batch of
alternatives, Taylor asked Sherwood which one he preferred.
'When I told him I preferred the green one, Graham threw
me a look, the kind of expression when you ask for a favour,
and said, "Can you wear the red one? It will keep Rita happy."
It didn't really matter to me what colour I wore. Goalkeeping
kits have changed a lot since then, and some of them are
horrendous. I looked like a pillar box all in red, and Tony Coton
refused point-blank to wear it, but flinging yourself around in
the mud isn't a fashion show. It didn't bother me.'

Sherwood was more interested in the advance of technology
where goalkeeping gloves were concerned. Like Pat Jennings,
the Northern Ireland legend who began his career at Vicarage
Road, Sherwood had hands like saucepans and the cotton green
gloves he used to wear at the start of his career were neither
use nor ornament. He even saw opposition keepers wearing
gardening gloves.

Sherwood felt empowered when manufacturers produced
gauntlets which aided safe handling and a modicum of
protection, but in the last weeks of his Watford career he was to

be denied a return to Wembley and an opportunity to lay to rest the ghost of Andy Gray. To lose one keeper with a busted digit in the fortnight before an FA Cup semi-final was unfortunate. To lose two was plain freakish, if not actually scary.

The Hornets had reached the last four with a workmanlike third-round win against non-League Maidstone on a heavily-sanded pitch, a narrow but deserved victory against Chelsea in front of the live TV cameras at Vicarage Road, an epic trilogy against obdurate Third Division underdogs Walsall and a marvellous quarter-final at Arsenal, where Watford's showcase for destructive wingers and resilience was partially obscured by a controversial climax.

Safely cocooned in mid-table, the season boiled down to a semi-final against Tottenham at Villa Park, a thankless 100-mile migration when Highbury would have made more sense as a neutral venue. But ahead of the campaign's defining Cup tie, providence dealt Taylor a cruel hand, and for once – possibly the only time in the messiah's original decade in charge at Watford – he fumbled the cards left available to him.

When first-choice Coton's season was ended by a broken thumb, fractured in two places after he parried a powerful shot from Luther Blissett in training, Watford were relieved that Sherwood was available to provide experienced cover. And although a gung-ho 4-3 defeat at Charlton, followed by a distracted and impoverished 3-0 loss at home to Queen's Park Rangers 48 hours later, was not the stuff of building confidence for Sherwood, there remained a blithe optimism that the Hornets would get it right when it mattered at Villa Park.

In the background, however, were unsettling signs that a storm was brewing. Taylor was concerned that Watford were unable to sell their full 20,000-ticket allocation for the semi-final, and feared a decade of upsetting the applecart was now giving way to a sense of entitlement and a comfort zone. And as if by magic, in the week leading up to the semi-final, stories surfaced in the establishment press that media tycoon Robert Maxwell, who already owned Derby County, was lining up an attempted takeover of Watford. It was like reading the Grim Reaper was coming to your birthday party.

And then, unbelievably, the injury curse struck again. Watford had decamped to Lilleshall in rural Shropshire – the national football centre before the Football Association built St George's Park – to prepare for Spurs. The change of scenery appeared to be uplifting until Sherwood, diving to his left in a shooting-practice drill, caught his little finger in the ground and dislocated it badly, almost at a right angle. Immediately, he knew it was potentially serious in terms of playing in the semi-final.

If having no fit goalkeepers for the biggest game of the season sounds eerily familiar, younger supporters who recall the final day of the 2012-13 season will recognise the photofit of an emergency. Gianfranco Zola's attempt to win automatic promotion at the first attempt floundered, and then expired, when Manuel Almunia was injured in the warm-up and his understudy Jonathan Bond was poleaxed in a sickening collision with team-mate Ikechi Anya after Leeds striker Dominic Poleon's cynical shove had set them on an irrevocable collision course. Poor Jack Bonham, who had answered an SOS from the stands minutes before kick-off, was unready for the trauma that unfolded.

A dislocated little finger may not sound serious, but it affects a surprising number of everyday functions, from holding a steering wheel to washing your hair in the shower, and Sherwood's damaged digit needed resetting in hospital – and the nearest one was almost an hour away at Telford.

'The key with dislocations is to get the joint reset as quickly as possible, so the delay wasn't great because the swelling takes hold,' says Sherwood. 'Fortunately, the glove gave me more protection than the flimsy things we used to wear and we managed to keep it iced. Once the finger was straightened out, I always thought I was going to make it.'

Taylor, forced to seek cover for Sherwood, had few alternatives to explore because the transfer window had closed and the only avenues open to him were players out of contract or those already registered on the books at Vicarage Road. He sounded out 41-year-old Jennings about coming out of his short-lived retirement to take a curtain call against his former club, and sent 45-year-old former Arsenal 'Double' winner Bob Wilson – by now presenting sport on TV – a distress flare.

Both veterans politely declined the offer, and although Watford had high hopes of their hugely promising 16-year-old youth-team keeper, Taylor felt it would be unfair to throw David James into the line of fire on such a big occasion. It would be another two years before James made his first-team debut and his abundant talent went on to command a seven-figure transfer fee.

With time running out, Taylor found emergency cover in the unlikely setting of an Ebbw Vale wine bar, where Hornets chief executive Eddie Plumley's son, Gary, ran the front of house. Plumley had performed capably against Watford in the Fourth Division for Newport County ten years earlier, and as a free agent he was available to sign non-contract forms. When Plumley hooked up with the Hornets squad, Taylor was impressed with his attitude in training, but the general consensus among the players was that Sherwood would play against Tottenham if he was passed fit.

'On the Saturday morning of the game, it's wet and windy, it's horrible, but I go through my routines, do some work on crosses and it's all fine,' says Sherwood in his unhurried recollections of a momentous day. 'Then, at the end of the session, Graham asked me to lie on the ground, with my injured hand outstretched, and he kicked a ball against it as hard as he could. There was no discomfort, and I told him, "Yeah, it's fine. No problem." I went back to the hotel feeling chipper and told Steve Sims, my roommate, "I've made it." Then there was a knock at the door and our physio, Billy Hails, said the gaffer wanted a word in his room. I just thought he was going to confirm I was playing, and at first there was no sign of anything to the contrary. He asked me, "How is it?" and I replied, "It's fine." That's when he dropped the bombshell. "Well, I can't tell you the reason, but I'm not going to play you." I was so shocked, I couldn't even speak. I didn't have a go at him or anything.

'When I went back to my room and told Simsy the news, he looked as startled as me and he said, "So this wine waiter is playing in goal instead of you?" Of course, I wished Gary all the best, and hoped that Graham had pulled a masterstroke by picking him, but after the warm-up one of the coaching staff came over to me and muttered, "I hope he plays better than he warms up."

'I don't think I've ever felt as bad watching a game of football as I felt that afternoon. It was just horrible, wishing I was somewhere else, and of course it was a terrible result.'

Taylor's confidence in Plumley, as it transpired, was misplaced. He was a bag of nerves. From Tottenham's first meaningful shot, a speculative effort from distance by Clive Allen, the wine-bar sommelier could not hold on and Steve Hodge devoured the rebound. Plumley was blameless when Allen tried his luck again two minutes later, and the debutant was stranded by a wicked deflection off John McClelland, but even the stealthiest contraband dealer should not have been able to smuggle a cross-shot between keeper and near post, as Hodge did to make it 3-0. As a contest, it was over before the interval, Watford lost 4-1 and Sherwood's dream of returning to Wembley, to complete unfinished business, evaporated faster than the bouquet of a decanted cabernet sauvignon.

'On the Sunday morning, I got a call from a guy on the *News of the World* offering me money to slag off Graham, but I wasn't interested. I told the fella, "Look, all I can say is that I was fit enough to play, but if you are looking for someone to trash my manager for the last ten years, you've come to the wrong guy." Hurt as I was, after everything we had achieved together, I wasn't going to sell him down the river for 30 pieces of silver. But from one end of the spectrum – feeling on top of the world when we won promotion, qualified for Europe and reached the Cup final – I had gone to the other, where I really couldn't have felt any worse. When you are bumped aside by a guy who is not even a League goalkeeper for a major semi-final, you kind of get the feeling that your time is up.

'Graham did say to me, before we went our separate ways, that there was a specific reason why he left me out and he promised to tell me one day. Sadly, he passed away without ever divulging his secret, whatever it was, and now we'll never know. But it still doesn't change my opinion of him as a manager or person. It was one decision, from a moment in time, but I still love the guy. I go back to that game at Coventry in 1980, when we lost 5-0 and he could easily have binned me. He was a great man.'

Plumley bought a fridge with his one-off £250 match fee and Sherwood was recalled for the home game against Chelsea 72 hours later, which the Hornets won 3-1. But for Taylor, the non-event at Villa Park marked the beginning of the end. In his post-match interview, GT had reflected ruefully that he could not keep pulling rabbits from the hat to order, and in his final programme notes of the season, he dropped a heavy hint that his reign was coming to an end, assuring supporters that 'Watford will always be a part of me.' Within days, his disciples' worst fears were confirmed: Taylor had been approached to become the manager of relegated Aston Villa, and nobody at Watford – from chairman Elton John to the most fairweather fan – could find it in their hearts to deny him the prerogative.

Taylor was not only one checking out of Vicarage Road. After 269 appearances spread across 11 years, all four divisions and a wind-assisted goal, Sherwood brought the curtain down on his Watford career in a 1-0 win against Tottenham, barely a morsel of revenge for the Hornets' FA Cup semi-final defeat but a symbolic clean sheet nonetheless. He pinched the official teamsheet as a souvenir.

By the time he bowed out with a richly deserved testimonial against Heart of Midlothian 48 hours later, his last appearance in a Watford shirt, Sherwood knew he would be leaving Watford – and he was also in on Taylor's secret. 'I can't even remember if my contract was up or not, but Graham pulled me aside and told me in confidence he was on his way, and that it wouldn't be worth my while sticking around because the new guy coming in didn't rate me,' he says. 'He didn't say Dave Bassett was coming in to replace him, but he obviously knew who it was. One of his last acts as Watford manager was to look after me and make sure I got fixed up. That speaks volumes for him. I knew I was signing for Grimsby before Bassett had even arrived.'

Just as he did with Watford, Steve Sherwood won back-to-back promotions with Grimsby and he played in the FA Cup first round for Gainsborough Trinity at the age of 44. He only quit football when he gashed his knee on a brick lurking just beneath the surface of the pitch at Colwyn Bay and doctors told him he was lucky not to contract septicaemia. Since 1998, he has been a financial adviser.

Sherwood never made it back to Wembley as a player, where his bonus for reaching the FA Cup final in 1984 was £1,000, and he says there were only four League grounds out of the 92 where he never played – one of them being Elland Road, which still riles him because he supported Leeds United as a boy.

Oh, and in case it has slipped his memory, guess who was the referee who let off Brighton's Michael Robinson with only a booking for that blatant headbutt at the Goldstone Ground on New Year's Day in 1983? Yes, it was his old friend from the Cup final – John Hunting.

2

IAN BOLTON

BY OLIVER PHILLIPS

My Best Signing

It could be argued that Ian Bolton, former centre-half of the Vicarage Parish, is one of those slightly forgotten and underrated heroes of the most memorable era in the history of Watford FC. Effortlessly we recall the likes of Luther Blissett and Ross Jenkins but there were several players from that halcyon era who were far more than just members of a supporting cast.

Most certainly Ian Bolton was one of those. Yet, despite having all the qualities that go to make a legend, when Watford fans are asked to name their all-time best team, 'Bolts' is often eased aside along with Pat Rice and Steve Sherwood and replaced respectively by John McClelland, Nigel Gibbs and Tony Coton.

However, the all-time highest-placed team in Watford's history finished second in the top flight, leaving a number of illustrious football names trailing in their wake. And that team included Bolton, Rice and Sherwood and at no stage during that season did we ever consider them weak or the weaker links.

'I would tend to agree that possibly John McClelland was a better defender,' Bolton concedes, but he does not need to remind me that he was one of the key elements in the most attack-minded of teams Watford ever produced. Without Bolton, the Graham Taylor narrative would have been quite different.

The Hornets' achievements in 1977-87 are seared into the joyous collective memories of all who witnessed them and they cannot be diminished by the carping, censorious critiques from the self-appointed high priests of so-called cultured football. Watford were labelled with blinkered simplicity as playing 'kick and rush', 'the long-ball game', 'by-passing the midfield' and 'taking football back to the dark ages'. The more the critics grumbled and quibbled, the tighter became Taylor's band of brothers, whose subsequent achievements were forged in an aura of siege mentality.

To a large degree Watford's dressing room took on their chins all the epithets, which described them as purveyors of stone-age football, yet there was one player who was in reality the arch-villain in the minds of the purists: Ian Robert Bolton.

'In a way I am quite proud of that fact: being recognised as an integral part of the manner in which Graham Taylor wanted to play. If I am to have the label of the main protagonist, then so be it,' says Bolton, a man who was able to change defence into attack in a couple of blinks of a jaundiced critic's eye.

'They don't just hoof it. They hit the ball into the space where a colleague is heading. It is a true skill to hit a ball that distance with that accuracy,' observed one of Watford's earlier rivals, Graham Turner, whose Shrewsbury side headed the Hornets out of the Third Division.

Having played with and against the best in the game, John Barnes – who launched his career on the left wing of Watford's attack and gained England honours long before Liverpool 'discovered' him – was quoted as saying: 'Ian Bolton was the best striker of a ball I ever came across.'

'No. I didn't just hoof the ball up the pitch,' says Bolton still slightly offended by the reminder of the age-old suggestion. 'Of course there were occasions when I was under pressure and I got rid of the ball upfield. Every defender has done that in his time. But I was naturally two-footed and I could hit the ball 40 yards with some accuracy. They weren't clearances; they weren't hit and hope; they were passes.'

The accuracy was one important fact but so too was the trajectory. Many players have observed they have never seen a ball hit in the way Bolton invariably sent his passes forward. Cristiano Ronaldo would clear the wall with a driven free-kick with his instep. Bolton's trajectory was similarly uncanny: the ball winging its way like an arrow to Jenkins' or Blissett's chest, feet or head. Or into the space they were heading for. Contrary to the popular critique, the ball did not come down with snow on it. The ball sped through the air, rarely more than eight feet from the ground before gradually arcing down to its target. In short it was not the long ball down the middle but more often the long pass out to the wings, but the purists will forever deny it.

'One of my best-ever passes was one I hit 50 yards, with pace, some two foot off the ground, straight to Barnes's feet. I loved that. Then there was the one against Sunderland at Vicarage Road when we won 8-0. I hit that ball down the right wing from around our penalty area, putting a curve on it from left to right and it dropped into Cally's path. Nigel took it on a few steps and then crossed for Luther to climb and head home,' he recalls with justifiable pride.

Apart from those unable to remove the bias from their eyes, it was apparent Watford worked on the tactic, many days after training, harnessing Bolton's unique ability and turning defence into attack with one blistering strike of the ball to Jenkins' chest.

'Sometimes Luther would come short and I could play it to him some 20 or 30 yards. It was a pass not a punt or a hoof,' says the attack-minded centre-half, who came to take all Watford's free-kicks and penalties. Why? Because he could place the ball where they wanted it, even if it were 30 or 50 yards distance. 'I was quite proud about my ability to strike a ball so it was annoying to be described as hoofing it forward without purpose. I used to power in the penalties whereas Sam [Ellis] would place them,' he reminded me and, when I confessed that I had experienced apprehension whenever he took a spot-kick, in case the keeper accidentally got in the way, Bolton contends the thought had never crossed his mind.

I saw all but one of Bolton's Watford displays and can categorically say he hit long passes. It is 34 years since he last hammered a ball forward into the path of a sprinting forward at Vicarage Road but the fans still remember. As Bolton says: 'The things they remember are the drama and the excitement; the goals as we broke goalscoring records. They remember the skills of our more gifted players but they never, ever talk about hitting long, hit-and-hope balls. It never happened.'

Among the prized possessions in the Bolton household is a Christmas card signed by 'Graham and Rita'. Beneath the signature is a short message: 'Still pound for pound my best-ever signing.'

Bolton was delighted when he first read of Taylor making such a claim: 'When you think of all the signings he made, to call me the best was really incredible.'

That then is just part of the case for placing Ian Bolton up there alongside the notable but relatively limited list of Watford legends.

* * *

Amidst a montage of manifold memories, when Bolton reflects on his early career in football, two stand out clamouring for attention. The first sees him as a 14-year-old, fighting to hold back the tears, and the second is at Lincoln where he spent a month on loan.

'I remember looking at their manager, Graham Taylor, and telling myself that if I could somehow hang on to his coat-tails, I could have a good career in the game,' he recalls.

That was some nine years and just over 55 miles from where, as a young teenager, Bolton, picked up his boots and made a reluctant and sad departure from Leicester City's Filbert Street. He had taken the news badly. The Leicester-born youngster had been training two nights a week at the ground, seeing the likes of his heroes Gordon Banks and Frank McLintock. Then one evening, he was told not to come for training any more. He was not going to be good enough. The man who was to stride with great authority across the Vicarage Road pitch during the most halcyon of Watford eras was heartbroken at the age of 14 after being informed he was not going to make it in professional football . . . as a left-winger.

'Yes, I was a left-winger in those days. I had been from the very start. After that setback I played for Mid-Leicester in the English Schools Trophy. I was fortunate to play at Southampton and score a hat-trick. Birmingham City came in and offered three of us apprenticeships,' he recalls. Yet the future all-time Watford hero steered an erratic course to Vicarage Road, overcoming further reverses.

'My father encouraged me in everything. He was an amateur footballer and cricketer. I played cricket and football whenever I could and, at one stage, it was a case of whether I would join Leicestershire CC or Birmingham FC. Although I opted for football, I still played cricket whenever I could.'

After a few years at Birmingham he tried to force the issue: 'At the age of 17 I told them they either offered me a professional contract or they sacked me. They sacked me,' he adds, seeing the humour of it now but recalling how he caught the train home to Leicester and loitered outside the front gate until finally plucking up his courage to enter his house and tell his parents what had transpired.

Now he was a redundant left-winger but admits he had only himself to blame: 'I had found out about drink and girls and I was smoking heavily. I got lost, so being sacked was the kick up the backside I needed.'

He was not out of work for long. Within a week he was playing for a boys' club that represented Notts County. He was selected as a centre-forward, performed really well and, after considering an offer from top-flight West Brom, opted to sign for County for £12 a week, as a striker. Breaking into a useful County first team was not easy, for Bolton was acting as understudy to the soon-to-be-famous Tony Hateley.

'I scored a lot of goals in the reserves but could not really break into the first team. Then one day I suffered from a slipped disc and my form dipped,' he says, recalling his third reincarnation as a footballer. 'As they were short of available defenders, the manager, Jimmy Sirrell, asked me to play centre-half. I did well but the regular pairing were the impressive David Needham and Brian Stubbs in the centre of defence, so opportunities were limited.'

When a young Lincoln manager, Graham Taylor, took him on loan for a month, Bolton saw the light.

'It was unbelievable at Lincoln. Boothy, Wardy and Sam were there and the organisation, the approach, the camaraderie were truly amazing,' he recalls. 'I was just in awe of Graham. I very quickly realised he was going to the top. He didn't have the money to sign me at Lincoln but then he moved to Watford and came in for me.'

It is said some defenders sustain a nosebleed when they penetrate deep into the opposition's half but that was not the case with Bolton. Having played on the wing and as a centre-forward, he was confident when making forward incursions. That proved to be extremely useful when he joined attack-minded Watford.

'That summer in 1977, I went round the one-way system in Watford and was so busy looking for the signposts, I drove up someone's backside. I got to the ground and Graham turned up in a tanned leather coat, looking like a used-car salesman. No disrespect: I came because of Graham, not because of Watford. So I met Graham, we agreed everything and that was the start of my and our incredible journey.'

It is a journey that is often revisited for those who worked with and under Taylor. That was so evident at the wake after his passing, for his charges of yesteryear indulged in a succession of nostalgic moments as the years just rolled away. As Bolton wrote in the condolence book: 'Gaffer! How could you have passed away? Do I not like that. Love you.'

For most, Taylor was held in reverence long after they left Watford.

Taylor's Convert

Back in 1977, Bolton was already converted to Taylor, his ideals and the way of playing the game.

'His team replicated him,' says the man who went on to make 288 appearances in just over six seasons, scoring 36 goals (including 11 penalties) under the manager they referred to as GT or the Gaffer. 'His teams were honest and full of drive. He had his morals and he was determined but he also made so many good decisions. Think about appointing Tom Walley as youth-team coach or bringing in Bertie Mee as assistant manager. They were spot-on decisions: strokes of genius.

'What is sad about Graham is that some people never recognise what you have got until you have gone. He was years ahead of his time in so many aspects but all the critics would go on about was their belief he was turning back the clock. He was an innovator and a pleasure to work for and with. They were very special days and he was a very special man,' says Bolton.

Yet Taylor was forced to defend his new £12,000 signing after Bolton played in a pre-season friendly against Oxford. 'It looked as if he could not head a ball and I was thinking, "Come on, lad, you can play better than that." I imagined Watford fans watching that game wondered what sort of berk I was, paying out £12,000 for him,' said Taylor.

Bolton reflects on that first season: 'I think I was pencilled in to replace Alan Garner, who was very popular with the fans. It did not help that I started shakily yet, as it turned out, we became regular partners. I never played with Sam. Initially I played in front of Alan and Sam, sweeping up in front, a bit like Chelsea did under Conte. Then I dropped back.

'Alan Garner was one of the best-looking footballers I have ever played with. He was a superb, quick athlete and maybe when I was brought in to replace him there was possibly a bit of animosity towards me as Alan was one of their favourite players. I could see why, yet I thought we formed a very good partnership for two number sixes.'

Alan Garner agrees: 'In the main I attacked the ball and Ian swept up but it depended on the occasion and the opposition. I think we had a good partnership. Bolts and Sam were both great guys but I could never understand why Taylor played Ian at centre-half. He could strike the ball and pass so well, I thought he should have been deployed further forward.'

When Taylor announced his first two signings – Bolton and Ellis – he described them as the ugliest and meanest centre-halves in the division.

'Just to clear that one up: I was the mean one,' Bolton smiles fondly at the memory. 'If you stood Sam by the fire in your house, the kids would never get burned.'

There is further evidence on that point. Towards the end of the season, Bolton picked up a record number of bookings, which was not part of Taylor's thinking. The manager fined players who were booked for dissent and would fine a player even if the referee had not punished what Taylor knew was a bad tackle.

'I got summoned to Lancaster Gate and the Gaffer came with me. I remember walking in and seeing a long table and elder statesmen sitting there in judgement. The Gaffer proceeded to defend me, explaining I had been bought as a centre-half and forced to play in midfield, but they didn't take any of that into consideration. I was suspended and fined a fiver, but those two weeks cost me. They had brought in a crowd bonus and our next game was Southend at home with nearly 19,000 there. I was suspended and I was gutted.

'However, driving back from the FA Panel, I stated that I would never get booked again. Graham turned to me and replied, plainly annoyed, that if I lost that meanness I would be gone. So I was the mean one.'

On occasions Taylor would pull Bolton and Ellis to one side. 'There was nothing devious about it. He wanted his captain on the pitch to represent him but he also wanted others to assert themselves. As we got through the divisions, Dennis Booth, myself, Steve Harrison and Pat Rice were among the many different characters we had.

'Look at the recent Arsenal team. There were no characters or winners. You need those type of players. You could have 11 George Bests and not win anything. It is about getting the mixture right. Tom Walley had some fantastically gifted players going through his hands but, as he said, ability alone will not get them there. You need consistency, drive and the will to win.'

On mention of the club's youth-team boss, Bolton recalls playing against him when the Welshman was at Orient: 'What a strong, uncompromising player he was with a tremendous left foot. Tom was a perfect lieutenant for the Gaffer: resolute, he knew what he wanted and he was honest. That was Tom and

GT. Every single person who played with and under Tom will not have a bad word said against him. We got on really well. He would tell you the way it was. He would jump on you if you didn't do what was required.

'Look at the job he did, culminating in winning the FA Youth Cup against Man United, who had Norman Whiteside and Mark Hughes in their side.

'The other point about Tom was that every team at Watford played the same way so a young player could slot in without a problem. He knew what was expected of him.'

There were several examples of players recruited to the Watford cause who did not fit in with the dressing-room culture, the style of play and the general philosophy. Names such as John Stirk, Ray Train and Mick Henderson come to mind.

'Joining a new club, you have to try to get used to a different philosophy. You are trying to adapt to a certain way of playing. If things had not gone well and not been taken on board by the players, it could have gone the other way, I suppose. It never entered my head at the time and I am sure it never entered Graham's mind.

'I think the Fourth Division was about accepting and adapting to a completely different type of football. I, along with the rest, had been aware of bits here and there, but not the whole package.'

Taylor managed to imbue his charges with the basics of his concepts and ensure that they implemented them.

'They were playing the same way at Lincoln. In the very early days of training at Watford, I remember the Gaffer walking out with an A4 book. I saw a little of it but every page was filled with details of how to play in given situations. We only had a short period of time to get used to it but it is a massive misconception that all we did was bash it long. Mind you, when you watch some of the really skilful teams trailing in the last ten minutes, they start hitting it long and hopeful.

'He had everything worked out and he knew it would work. Very soon we developed that in-built confidence. I know I, along with many others, bought into his drive and ambition to go to the top. I don't think I doubted him one little bit on the way to the top. To play in a side in which every player knows what he is doing; it was unbelievable. The further Luther and Ross got away, the further we at the back moved forward to make the team compact. In effect, we all did the same amount of running as a block.'

Pressing Game

For those who did not witness Watford's speedy climb, the contents of that A4 book would be illuminating.

'The game was about many things, not least winning the ball back in the opposition's half. They would be moving forward and if you dispossessed them, they would be vulnerable. So we worked the opposition defenders, either regaining possession or forcing them into hurried passes. It was called closing down. Now they call it a high-pressing game and talk about it as if it were something new. We were doing just that 40 years ago. It was a key element in our game but all people seemed to note was me hitting 30- and 40-yard passes,' Bolton points out.

Watford under Taylor were keen to turn the opposition defence, with the strikers running in an arc as soon as the likes of Bolton gained possession.

'If you are playing in the opposition half, they are going to find it very difficult to score. Our forwards were very mobile, undertaking those cross-overs as we looked to turn the defenders, sometimes by a chip over the top for Luther but not an upfield punt: not hitting and hoping and then chasing.

Defenders can do well when they are right in behind the forward but if you turn them, they are in trouble. The one thing they do not like is pace, and the likes of Luther had that.'

Bolton points out that Watford's philosophy also included maximising the number of goal attempts: 'Graham had people compiling statistics at every match. How many shots, how many crosses, how many second balls did you win? He was challenging players to produce what was required and what the team required.

'My long clearances to Ross or Luther helped to compress the opposition in their half and by pressing we could force them into errors. All the players were told to look for the forward pass first. Only if it wasn't on did we pass sideways.

'Graham had statistics for everything. As it worked out, Luther would need so many attempts in order to score a goal. To equate to that you needed Barnesy and Callaghan sending over a certain minimum number of crosses. From memory, Dalglish needed 7.9 attempts in order to score and Luther would need a few more.'

Other players have testified that they were drilled incessantly so that at any frozen moment in the game, the players knew exactly where their colleagues were. Dennis Booth recalled they practised 60 corners one morning, drilling home how the players should react when the ball was hit into a certain area.

Bolton admits: 'I suppose you could call it regimented but he got the basics right first. Football is a simple game and I think too many coaches complicate it in an attempt to justify their jobs. Graham inherited a decent chassis of a car and put various parts in it to make it work properly. He wanted that car to work at 100 per cent, maximising the potential of those parts.

'As we travelled up the League, certain parts were replaced with better ones and the original 1000cc car was improved to

1500, then 2000 and finally 2500cc. The basic shape remained the same but gradually the potential grew.

'But it was not that Graham disliked flair. He felt we did not express that enough in the Fourth Division and we improved on it but, for Graham, flair was something you produced in the opposition's half. He encouraged Luther, Barnsey and Cally to do so. Win the ball, get it forward and then try and torment the defence: that was his belief. But they had to be prepared to get crucified by the boss if there was no end-product to their flair.'

Bolton is one of many who firmly believe Taylor enhanced their ability as players and as men: 'I cannot speak highly enough of him. He had his own moral code and he kept to it and expected you to do the same. We improved as men, taking on responsibility. He involved us with the community right from the outset. He also made sure we kept our feet on the ground. We had to take our kit home and clean it every day. He did not want or let us get carried away.'

Watford's players had to commit to community work but, contrary to the common belief, the hours were not logged in their contracts back in 1977.

'It was a very rewarding experience. Imagine going to hospital and seeing the reaction of children if you gave them Christmas presents. It also brought home to you how revered you were with the fans. I think players are more insulated from the public now, not just by the excessive wages and the circles they move in, but the way football is.

'I remember Graham went to the house of a young fan who had died. He did so to commiserate with the family, who then took him up to show him the bedroom. He was really amazed to see how much Watford memorabilia there was. He was very moved and told us all about it.

'In those days you were still within accessible reach of fans. You might earn three times more than the average supporter but those community visits made you increasingly aware of what being a footballer meant to the local community.

'Anyone that knew Graham Taylor and came into Watford FC would come into the club and know that Graham ran it from top to bottom. You could see his character and his stamp reflected over the whole club and in the way he got the club to put back into the community.

'We were told to do the community stuff and I think every one of us enjoyed it. Of course, being successful on the pitch helped us establish that rapport but even when we struggled in the old second tier, we still had that rapport with the fans. It was a two-way thing: they were pleased to see us and we were pleased to see them.'

Tactics and pattern of play apart, Watford's players were presented with many new concepts.

'Initially, you had a lot to learn and take on board, such as how you were to conduct yourselves. There was an immense amount of work. You had to work hard and, when it came to going out at nights, play hard if you liked but within his moral codes. He did not object to you going out and having a few drinks but he would know all about it if anyone went over the line. I think he moulded people as men, so that they could become the best they could be on and off the field.

'At the early stage, he was intent on involving the local town and catchment area, where the local supporters came from. He had that blueprint. The more you think back, [the more you see] he had this plan for the whole thing. He probably had his plan for Elton.'

But much of this was developed behind the scenes. We noticed more players were attending local functions but our main focus was on the team and what the new manager could achieve with a group that had been underperforming for three or four seasons. Bolton believes Taylor improved a number of players, playing to their strengths and working on how to reduce the impact of their limitations.

'Look how he improved Ross Jenkins, who couldn't trap a bag of cement when I first came to the club. The ball used to bounce off him. His control was not good but Graham got me and Ross to stay behind and I would knock 40- or 50-yard balls forward to him. Ross would run to meet them and try to trap them on his chest or with his feet. We kept at it and Ross really improved. Years down the line I am able to state that Ross was the best centre-forward this club ever had. His control with his chest was brilliant. He led the line superbly. The improvement in control was down to Graham.

'When you think of us – like the Dirty Dozen, a group of misfits, mavericks, assembling at Watford for pre-season training – it was a remarkable achievement to not only mould us into champions of the Fourth Division but also to continue moving upwards,' says Bolton. 'He did not rate Watford or the players before he took over but – with the addition of Sam Ellis, me, Dennis Booth and Brian Pollard – he turned that squad into a real force. But they did have some good players there already. He improved Bobby Downes, playing him further forward and utilising his great left foot. A really nice fella who proved to be a real asset.'

One of the players Taylor brought in was Brian Pollard, who arrived from York City midway through Taylor's first season in charge with high hopes but made only a limited impact.

'He was a real character, really hard-working but a little inconsistent with his crosses. He loved to drink but he became one of those players the Gaffer would chastise in front of everyone and use him as an example to make a lot of points. Within time, Polly contributed to our success and, for all that chastisement, was upset when he had to leave. It was that sort of dressing room.'

Among the players Taylor inherited was Keith Mercer, whom they called 'Bamm-Bamm' after the *Flintstones* character.

'You think of those four Division Four strikers: Ross, Luther, Keith and Alan Mayes. You could pick any two of those four. They were superb players; all different in their own way. The casualties were Mayesy, who was so skilled, and Keith who was big and strong and would run through a brick wall, which was not Mayesy's game. Nor was it his game to run past and behind the defence, which the Gaffer wanted players to do. Keith would put his head in and get it kicked off, which can result in a lot of injuries and he paid a high price for his bravery. The Gaffer loved his attitude: "Going in horizontal" he called it.'

In the lower divisions there was some debate over the qualities of Keith Pritchett and Taylor's subsequent signing Steve Harrison.

'Keith Pritchett had a superb left foot, was a tremendous athlete and was a very, very good player in my opinion. Obviously the Gaffer saw it differently. You could see why he liked and preferred Steve Harrison, but look at Keith and put him in a different team, he might have been an even better player. Maybe he had more than the Gaffer wanted whereas Harry was what he needed at the time. Keith was a lovely fella whereas Harry was off the wall: a lovely fruit bat and one of the funniest men I have ever met.

'Another player was chirpy Trevor How. He never quite established himself under Graham but he had the ability. Then there was Boothy, who I played with at Lincoln. He was a brilliant continuity player, kept things flowing on the pitch and was an unbelievable character in the dressing room. When it came to confidence, his was off the scale. He knew what his role was. He knew what his limitations were, as we all did our own limitations, but I think he thought of himself as a real midfield player. I was really close to Dennis and we got on fabulously.

'But talking about limitations, being a successful and effective footballer was all about realising them and not exposing them.'

When looking to the players Taylor inherited, he was extremely well placed for goalkeepers.

'Andy Rankin was unbelievable,' Bolton claims. 'One of the best shot-stopping keepers I ever played with. A fantastic character, with the driest sense of humour I have ever come across and a mouthful of false teeth.

'The overwhelming memory of Andy was the game at Man United when we were in Division Three. We had taken the lead and, late on, Gordon McQueen sent this header for a certain equaliser up in the top corner. I couldn't see Andy Rankin so I "knew" they had scored then but, like Superman, Andy came flying across and this hand tipped the ball away. It was a really stunning save. They don't get better than that. I walked past him and said: "Andy, could you not have held onto that?" He was spitting feathers.'

Bolton had to take goal-kicks because kicking long was not Rankin's strength.

'Steve Sherwood played all the way up the League. He was quiet until rattled; a lovely fella, a monster of a guy who had to establish himself. Shirley grabbed the opportunity despite the Gaffer bringing in Eric Steele, who was a tremendously agile keeper, shot-stopper and confident character but couldn't consistently dislodge Steve.'

A smile comes to Bolton's face when he recalls a dressing-room incident. Sherwood attempted to take a picture of the squad with his new camera, which had a pop-up flash: 'The flash goes off and we start to move but Shirley is still there, rooted to the pose. He had the flash too close to his forehead and it fused the skin, grafting the camera on. He just said: "Things keep happening to me." And they did.'

Another strong and influential player on the books when Taylor arrived in 1977 was Roger Joslyn.

'He was a strong character,' Bolton stresses. 'He was 100 per cent whole-hearted. He would go through two brick walls for you. He typified what the manager wanted from a midfield player: strong, determined and wouldn't back down to anyone and anything. Did a tremendous job for the team.'

The recruitment of Booth from Lincoln three months into the season, proved to be a masterstroke, for not only was the player an unsung continuity man in midfield, he also leavened the dressing-room intensity with large dollops of humour.

Says Bolton: 'You can never underestimate the contribution made by Boothy and, later, Steve Harrison as well. They were so funny. It made going into the dressing room that much more enjoyable. On occasions it broke the tension. I suppose we were nervous as we went into that first season and I think the Gaffer was nervous as well. He had turned down a First Division club to come to Fourth Division Watford. He had set himself up as a target but also I think he worried whether the players would take it all on board and make it work.'

Bolton does not remember too much about games but remembers incidents and the aura of the time: 'I found it hectic and I like to think I settled down a lot more and started to play the way the Gaffer and I wanted me to play. We went on a successful run showing that the team was grasping his tactics and pattern of play. After those first few games in the Fourth Division, we hit the top and never looked back. He said at the outset that we would win the title by ten points and we did it with 11.'

Yet the ease with which Watford dominated Division Four belies the intensity of the work that went on behind the scenes.

'There was a lot of hard work involved in training. We worked so hard before the season started and it never let up.

Yes, he told us he was going to the top and wanted to know who was going with him. Well, I was already committed. He kept on at us and was constantly urging us to improve. I must admit, I was never one for physical training. I really enjoyed training with a ball at my feet but I dreaded Tuesdays. We would start by doing weights, then doggies – sprinting back and forth to targets over 20 yards in short, sharp, physical bursts – for an hour, which was murder. Then you would do a 12-minute run around the dog track or pitch. Joslyn and Barnes would get in 12 laps; me, Steve Sherwood and Simsy would get in six. Perhaps I am exaggerating but it felt like that.'

Taylor had a firm belief that the stomach was the core to your fitness and well-being.

'We did a lot of abdominal training, on the ground or bench and ultimately with Tom Walley throwing a medicine ball against your stomach. It paid dividends. But I hated that. Then we'd drive, [already] feeling absolutely shattered when we parked by Cassiobury Park.

'We would walk over to the start and would run five miles, in which the Gaffer would take part. There was nothing more frustrating than seeing Roger Joslyn in the early days and later John Barnes going away while we had a heart attack at the back.

'John or Jos did it in 16 min; Gaffer would finish fourth and we would finish last in 22 minutes. That completed the training. Tuesdays were murder. But I can tell you this: I had never felt so fit, strong and healthy. It was an unpleasant necessity. It was necessary at the time to give us that strength. Graham was insistent that you should be able to physically achieve in the last minute of the game the same as you could in the first minute.'

Taylor believed you put 'fitness in the bank' in pre-season and that players would be able to draw upon it throughout the campaign. Occasionally, if fixtures allowed in the New Year, he would put the players through it again in order to 'top up the deposits of fitness'.

Watford out-ran, out-fought and out-played the majority of their rivals in Division Four as they powered through the season, losing just five League fixtures and only one at home.

'It was a big thing with the Gaffer to make sure we made playing at Vicarage Road a fortress. We wanted teams to fear taking us on. The opposition had the mindset they would settle for a 1-1 draw before they took the field.'

Captain Webb

Ian Bolton's move to Watford was to spark a name-change. That did not come until pre-season training in 1978, when he emerged from the shower and walked naked back into the dressing room. The shower had provided his hair with a centre parting. Dennis Booth looked at his naked colleague and said: 'You look like Captain Matthew Webb – the first man to swim the Channel.'

Bolton laughs at the memory: 'I wish he had called me donkey but Webb was his call and it stuck. Even I refer to myself as Webb. So does my wife. Some call me Webby but that name certainly caught on.'

Watford had arrived in Division Three as a well-trained commando force and, while Taylor would contend they were nowhere near the finished article, the players had the belief and confidence in their game sufficient to assert themselves and lead the table for much of the season. The manager, however, wanted to cater for greater flair, believing that quality was by-passed as he drilled his troops throughout the Fourth Division season.

'After winning the Division Four title the Gaffer was able to say, "yes, I have the right players," and we approached the Third Division with a lot more confidence. Your reputation went ahead of you. We led that division for quite a time. We were on a roll,' Bolton points out.

Yet the season produced an unexpected bonus. While the manager was looking at other strikers, Luther Blissett forced himself into the reckoning with two goals in the home League Cup tie against Newcastle United, in what was the first of several years of famous, pulsating Watford nights.

Taylor greeted Blissett's success with a dismissive but challenging comment: 'I have seen this all before. What we want is for him to do it consistently.'

Ross Jenkins had already started the season with 13 goals in the first 14 outings and Blissett came up with two uncharacteristic goals at Old Trafford. Unquestionably, Luther was one of the top stars, who epitomised the rise up the divisions but Bolton admits he was not converted initially.

'When I first saw Luther he was big, strong, brave, powerful with a great physique but raw. I think being at Watford and being with Graham was the making of him. I am not so sure he would have achieved what he went on to achieve had he not been at Watford. He played within a team and a system that played to his strengths. Look at Benteke, who went to Liverpool who did not play to his strengths. Then he went to Palace and that suited him because of the way they played.

'Luther would try forever. Luther and Ross were the perfect foil for each other. He became a very, very good player indeed. I could always rely on knowing where Luther or Ross would be. In fact, we could hit the ball blindly if the occasion demanded. Yes, even now I can see Boothy's clipped cross to Luther as he moved towards the penalty spot at Old Trafford for one of those goals.'

But Luther's double at Old Trafford to send Manchester United spinning out of the League Cup, catapulted the striker into national headlines and ultimately national recognition.

It was a classic example of what confidence can do for a player who came out from the dressing room after his headed double, saying: 'You know me. Two headed goals: it's ridiculous.'

'Back then, Luther had a head like a rugby ball. Unless you caught it with the right spot, [the ball] would go anywhere,' Bolton remembers. 'We were a goal down to Joe Jordan's strike and then we pulled back and took the lead with Luther heading them both. That was amazing. I remember the Gaffer being sarcastic during the interval and saying we were a goal down and had not done badly. We were expected to lose so it was OK. Then he turned and snarled at us to get out there and put some crosses and shots in. "Go out there and represent me properly," he said.

'It made so much difference to Luther. Then there was Andy's great save and we were through: headline-makers and giant-killers. It was one of those nights that went on for a little while. We had a few drinks that night: similar to the Southampton night a couple of years later. We did celebrate. As I say, the Gaffer wanted you to work hard and play hard within reason.'

Watford went on to lose only two of their next 20 games and the double-act of Luther and Ross continued to dominate the Third Division headlines. By Christmas, Watford looked near-certainties for promotion but then they started to draw matches and the momentum slowed.

By then, Bolton had suffered a setback. He had slipped a disc back in his Notts County days and Watford knew he had that vulnerability. His back played up again in the December and the centre-half was hospitalised.

'I was lying in hospital with a back injury when the Gaffer went out and bought Steve Sims for £175,000 – a Third Division record. He had already bought Ray Train for £50,000 a few weeks earlier and that had been a club record. The signing of

Simsy was quite a shock. I think, looking back, that was the last thing I needed, lying in bed with this back problem. Maybe at the time I did not appreciate it could have been the crossroads.

'I had slipped a disc cleaning my teeth. One of those unfortunate things is that every now and then it would catch you out. That was the gamble the Gaffer took when he bought me and he would take me out for two or three games a season to ease the problem. I was very fortunate in that I sustained a broken nose but not a broken arm or leg. I did not have hamstring or groin injuries or metatarsal injuries, which they get now. I can't remember anyone I played with getting a metatarsal injury.'

To say the least, he was at a low point: his career in jeopardy and his probable replacement already drafted in. However, it transpired that another centre-half, Sam Ellis, realised time was effectively being called on his playing career, and so Ian Bolton and Steve Sims became a very impressive partnership.

'We bedded in. He was a big character, but a big kid,' says Bolton. 'Everyone adored him within the dressing room. What you saw with Simsy was what you got. He wore his heart on his sleeve. He was a giant of a man with incredible shoulders and proved to be an absolute success. He was very easy to play with. Simsy was my favourite partner and I envied his ability in the air. You could totally rely on him. He'd definitely be the one you want in the trenches. In *Dad's Army*, he would have been Pike.'

Steve returns the compliment: 'I joined halfway through the Third Division. I tended to take the big, ugly ones: Cyrille Regis, Mick Harford types. It suited us both. He let me do the heading and he swept up around me. Webby was a great striker of a ball. We didn't say a lot, we just knew what was happening. It was one of Graham's things that we worked hard on the back four with Steve Harrison when he became coach.

'Webby had great feet. I thought the right was his best but he could pass with either of them. I signed for Watford when Ian was in his hospital bed with his back. As it happened, I stayed with him for a few weeks as well. Lovely fella; smoked like a trooper; had 15 sugars in his cup of tea . . . well, six or seven. He was always at the back in cross-country but he was quick enough on the pitch.

'It was a very successful partnership. I trusted him. We were solid. We never had any arguments.' They were to have one earnest discussion when Liverpool were beating Watford 3-0 at Anfield. Bolton was marking Dalglish and having trouble with it.

'I suggested we change and he take Ian Rush. Webby said: "No, I'm getting it." Getting it? I pointed out we were 3-0 down but he was determined to master it. I think that was the only real occasion when we were taken apart.'

The other recruit, Ray Train was signed as an example of Bolton's view that Taylor changed the parts on the Watford car in order to improve them. Bolton remembers: 'He was a very skilful, good, attacking player but found it difficult to adjust to the culture. Graham stayed with the format as much as possible when we got promotion to Division Two.'

* * *

There were many theories as to why Watford started to struggle towards the end of that 1978-79 season. From promotion favourites they slipped to the position of outsiders at one stage. Sims and Train were cup-tied and could not participate in Watford's superb run to the League Cup semi-final, where they bowed out to Brian Clough's Nottingham Forest.

'I remember we hit the bar, which would have made it 2-2 at their place if the ball had gone in. It rebounded and they went upfield and scored to make it 3-1. Forest paid us respect when they came to Vicarage Road in the second leg and closed the game down at 0-0. That was quite a compliment,' says Bolton.

The middle part of the season resulted in a 'cup team' and the 'league team' and some felt Taylor should have stuck with the side that took them to the top of Division Three. Indeed, following the first semi-final leg, Watford drew seven and lost one of the next nine games, allowing the rest of the pack to close in.

Watching from the sidelines, it seemed as if the 3-3 draw at home to Bury after leading 3-0 caused a lasting shock, for Watford and the crowd seemed on edge with a home lead after that. In the next ten games, Watford won only four, drawing two and losing four to leave them struggling, with Shrewsbury, Swansea and Gillingham looking the most likely to fill the three promotion spots.

One of the draws was at Gay Meadow, when Watford levelled the scores against the eventual division champions with a free-kick from Bolton: 'If memory serves me that was the first time we tried the "explosion" free-kick when we put a wall up in front of opposition's. Their fans were giving me stick but then I ran up, our wall dissolved and I scored. We used that ploy for years.

'I do remember that trip,' admits Bolton, who tends not to recall many individual games and goals. 'On the way up, we had left Vicarage Road soundly beaten at home by Colchester, and we were struggling to recapture the form we had enjoyed earlier in the season. The Gaffer got director Jim Harrowell to show his open wounds that he had to dress every day. He had picked them up in the desert campaign during the Second World War. Graham explained that people overcome setbacks and our problems were nothing compared to Mr Harrowell's. We drew at Shrewsbury that day when we were expected to lose.'

Watford rallied with a narrow home win over Chester before going to Hillsborough to take on Sheffield Wednesday, which Bolton remembers well too: 'I can remember us getting a penalty at 2-2 and I scored and ran behind the goal, celebrating in front of the Sheffield Wednesday supporters. That was a great win. Teams can have a wobble but we had chalked up two successive victories to put ourselves in with a shout.'

Watford had to wait nine days for the denouement and so Taylor took them to France and a match against Sochaux, which ended 0-0. They flew back on the Saturday and prepared for the final game, against Hull City at Vicarage Road on the Monday night. Hull had beaten them 4-0 earlier in the season and Watford paid them back with a 4-0 victory with goals by Jenkins, Blissett, Joslyn and a Bolton penalty.

'After the game, during the celebrations, I remember Elton sent out for 50 portions of fish and chips down in the boardroom. It sounds pathetic now but it was lovely back then. It is weird when you look back and think of some of the things. When we got promoted from Third to Second we got a gold disc for backing vocals on Elton's *Single Man* album. Elton wanted to buy each player an inscribed Rolex but the Gaffer would not allow him to. That typified his nature: feet on the ground, working-class attitude. His view was that you are in a privileged position, in a wonderful occupation but he always kept you grounded, trying to teach you lessons.

'I love Graham and really miss him, but it would look nice now to have an inscribed Rolex from Elton. I don't think we would have got carried away; it would have just been a nice memento.'

It was a superb season for Watford and Bolton who managed to squeeze between the two headline-makers in the fans' vote for Player of the Season, finishing second to 37-goal Jenkins and ahead of 28-goal Blissett.

Taylor reflected on the season and revealed that he knew Bolton was a good player: 'But I didn't realise how good he was until I worked with him. Ian has been outstanding and he is working on his main fault – that impetuosity that makes him go into challenges he cannot hope to win.'

Bolton certainly worked on that tendency and wiped it out of his game for the following season when, despite Watford struggling in Division Two, he gained his most treasured award: the *Watford Observer*'s Player of the Season Award 1980.

'I had been third, then second and frankly, in that first season in the second tier, I was in the form of my life. I was totally on top of my game. That is my most prized possession. The fans chose me.'

Only one trophy runs that close for Bolton: 'I was invited to the club to be designated a Watford Legend. That was only a few years ago, but that really touched me.'

Reaching the second tier produced its own problems and the Hornets struggled to come to terms with them after having had it pretty much their own way while climbing the League ladder over the previous two seasons. Taylor would later reflect he broke up the old side too quickly, for he sold Joslyn, Pollard, Mercer, Garner and Downes in the space of three months.

'Maybe in hindsight he did it too early but then again, the new men did not settle well. Micky Henderson was a great lad but never came to terms with the tactics and the culture and Wilfy Rostron was not a success,' contends Bolton.

'But then Graham pulled a masterstroke later, by putting him at left-back up against speed-merchant Clive Walker of Chelsea. I think we were stunned by that decision, to be fair. Then we were totally amazed by the impact he had. As a left-back, Wilfy was phenomenal. He had a good left peg, had played on the wing and had the advantage, like I had, of going from being a forward to a defender. I have to say, Wilf turned out to be the best left-back Watford ever had – hard, mean and nasty and he had an incredible jump. I'm glad Wilfy misfired when he first came to the club. Had he not done that he would have stayed

on the left wing and been replaced by Barnsey. The switch to
left-back was really a brilliant stroke.'

Although, initially, the recruitment of Henderson and Rostron
did nothing to improve the side, Bolton was impressed by the
other recruits: John Ward, Malcolm Poskett and Martin Patching.

'Malcolm! What a goalscorer. He had the most superb,
coolest finish I have ever seen. Then there was John Ward, who
I knew from Lincoln. He was not a No.9 but he knew the game.
He was good at holding the ball up and setting up attacks. He
was someone the Gaffer could always rely on in any position on
the field. Once again, a man with a really dry sense of humour
and a really funny bloke.'

But Bolton was most impressed with the midfielder signed
from Wolves: 'In life you meet people who have special qualities,
and Martin Patching's potential and future would have been
unbelievable. The way he played, he was a more modern-day
midfielder who had everything. I was ten yards away when his
ligaments snapped like a gun. I heard it. I was recovering from
a back injury and got close to him. If he'd stayed fit, he would
have had a long and very successful career.'

The Impossible Dream

Watford limped on in the 1979-80 season with Jenkins out
injured for three months and Blissett missing his partner.
Knocked out of the League Cup in the first round by Colchester,
Watford were now a scalp for the lower-division clubs and the
Hornets had a fright in the FA Cup when they only overcame
non-league Harlow 4-3 at Vicarage Road after falling behind.

'What a scare that was. We could have lost that game; instead
we went on to beat Wolves 3-0 at their place. They had Andy Gray,
John Richards and Emlyn Hughes. They were in the top flight.'

Watford bowed out 2-1 at home to Arsenal in the quarter-finals but four victories in their last six games put the outside threat of relegation behind them.

'Then Pat Rice came the next season. He was an unbelievable player to bring in. He had that experience: been there, done that, and Pat was old enough to realise what the Gaffer wanted. Not the quickest of full-backs, they said, but no one ever got the better of him.'

Watford had tasted success in the second tier but, says Bolton, 'I think we realised the next step that we were looking to take would be a lot more difficult than we had been used to.' Yet the Hornets might have gained a false impression in the 1980-81 campaign, with League Cup success over Southampton and Nottingham Forest.

'We went to Southampton in the first leg and it was a total embarrassment. They were top of the top flight and were a very good side. That 4-0 defeat was a massive shock to our system. We came across a slightly different quality of players. One of them, Nick Holmes, scored with a left foot from basically the halfway line. I think we got what we deserved.

'We still had the return leg but it was going to be difficult. You are not going to beat them 5-0: we knew that. They were top of the First Division. The Gaffer said: "Let's go out and beat them, just feel better and overall it will be one game each." As it turned out, it was just one of those strange, strange nights. Everything everyone tried, it just came off. Everyone played to the top of his game.

'I can remember the BBC newsreader saying "one moment, please" after reading the 7-1 result because he thought it was a misprint. As debilitating as the first game was, the second was the polar opposite. It did us a world of good. I just think it rejuvenated our belief, revitalised us and gave us the kick up the backside we needed,' he said of Watford's 7-5 aggregate win, in which he scored from the spot.

Then came Brian Clough's Nottingham Forest to be put to the sword 4-1. 'Ross scored a hat-trick. That was thoroughly deserved. We were on a high. They were great, great nights. We had so many of them.

'After that, we added to the squad with Pat Rice, Gerry Armstrong and "Little Legs" Les Taylor. I just thought Les was superb: hard-working, enthusiastic, never shirked a tackle and I thought he and subsequently Jan Lohman were superb together. Jan had a lot more skill and ability than he was given credit for. With his moustache he might have looked like Adolf Hitler, but Jan and Les were the sort you wanted in the trenches alongside you. But Les was like he was on Duracell. In today's game you see them count the miles or kilometres covered. How many did Les cover?

'Another midfielder, Kenny Jackett, typified the extra quality we took on board as we progressed through the divisions. You are trying to improve the quality of those players but retain the combativeness and add the little bit of skill. Kenny came through the ranks so he absolutely knew what was required of him. He had a tremendous left peg. It was really sweet and he was certainly not afraid to tackle.'

Taylor was pleased with his two signings but it was the third, Gerry Armstrong, who really upped the manager's expectations.

Bolton understands the sentiment: 'Gerry obviously was a renowned name. It was synonymous with what Graham was trying to do with the team: improving the quality. He was meeting the higher expectations of the fans who were were expecting progress. I think it reflected the club's ambitions. He was a tremendous signing and had the capabilities to help the club improve.

'Ross went through a difficult time with injury and went over to Washington. We stayed with him for six weeks in the summer. I thought it was only natural Ross went. Gerry had massive shoes to fill. Very much a confident, impact player, Gerry was wholehearted and an absolute beast. He was a fighter, which is what you needed in the squad. Gerry would physically beat you up. You could never expect that from Roscoe.'

Bolton saw the clash of personalities between Taylor and Ross as understandable: 'The Gaffer got most things right but he was wrong there. He was looking to replace Ross and put him on the list. It proved to be a mistake.'

It was not the happiest season for Bolton, however. He was to be out for four months when his back problem flared up again. 'I had one disc in the lower back that was worn, the next was knackered and the third was worn. I went to Harley Street and they recommended a then-revolutionary procedure which they had never tried on a sportsman before – they injected dynamite in my spine. Sounds bizarre but the discs disintegrated and the rest fused with my spine.

'I had scored in my last game before the op in October and I scored on my first match back, 28 games later. They said they were effectively injecting me with arthritis, but all I wanted was to get back. Now I know what they meant about arthritis but it is not bad and I manage it.'

Bolton's return coincided with Watford's run of eight wins and three draws from their last 15 games to finish ninth in the second-tier table – then the highest position the Hornets had ever achieved in the club's history. As a result there was a growing confidence about putting the struggling days in Division Two behind them. But when Taylor announced before the first match, 'It is time we were moving on,' did he really mean promotion to the top flight? Clearly he did and – with

Callaghan blooded and Barnes proving to be a stellar youth signing – Watford began to make real progress.

'I think every season you start off with general positivity. Maybe we needed a season or two to get used to the type of players, the better players you are coming up against and also the better managers. I think as a team we were quite quick learners. Looking back, we destroyed them and the more you get used to playing against them, the more we learned what we really had to do.'

Taylor encouraged and cajoled and occasionally lost his temper.

'His rollickings could be fearsome. We walked into the dressing room, and if the vein in his neck was throbbing that was a tell-tale sign. On one occasion he swiped the table with tea on it. Everything came off. It has gone all over me and I said: "Have you got any sugar?"

'He was always thrown by such comments. He pointed his finger at me and said: "Sugar. You want sugar." He was lost for a retort. But you also knew when he did compliment you, that meant so much. Generally, he was right when he lost it.'

Another new recruit was Steve Terry who came through the ranks. 'He had a tremendous future but found his path blocked by me and Simsy. A giant, brave and a lovely lad, Steve should have achieved more in the game.'

Bolton remembers the promotion season well. 'It took us a little bit longer to settle and realise that, once again, we deserved to be where we were and were part and parcel of that division. We started to really believe it just after Christmas. You have played every team once and generally you know you can beat them again. The belief was there and people had taken the pattern of play on board. It takes time. With some players it was like trying to teach a left-handed man to write right-handed. But we had Ross back, with Luther and Gerry weighing in as well. We were a force in the division.

'Then we got to the Wrexham match at home and Ross scored two. We had done it: won promotion to the top flight – total elation and on cloud nine. I threw my shirt away because I was so carried away. I wish I hadn't. I would have liked to have kept it.'

It seemed hard to comprehend that little Watford were going to mix it with the big boys, but Bolton says that the players believed it from the start: 'We knew the system could work against the so-called better teams. We had proved that in cup matches and we believed it would work in the higher echelons. Not only did it work but we really enjoyed playing that way.'

Bolton, along with Les Taylor, had finished ever-present in the League but had also enjoyed two memorable FA Cup victories against top-flight Manchester United and West Ham. He had also netted eight goals including a bizarre 60-yarder at Rotherham.

'I was interviewed by one of my earlier heroes, Derek Dougan, on the radio after that game and I told him I had run back to collect the ball deep in my half, moved forward and spotted the keeper off the line . . . Then I cracked up. I was unable to maintain my pretence. In fact I had launched it forward, hoping to find Ross's head. The wind caught it and took it over the keeper and into the net. The important thing was that we won on a wet, miserable day when we played abysmally.

'I do recall scoring a cracking free-kick against Luton, which was extra enjoyable, but my best goal had an element of luck. Coming out of defence against Norwich, I gave the ball to Cally and for some reason decided to overlap him. I called out "Yes," while waving my hand down low as a "no" at the same time. Cally opted to pass it to me. I was ten yards inside the touchline and I did actually look up. The keeper was perhaps a yard or two off his near post but the reason I decided to shoot was that I was knackered by my run. It looked a really stunning goal and I still have the video. It rocketed off my foot and straight into the top corner. I did aim at the goal, I must point out. I just hit it so hard.'

* * *

And so the target once dubbed 'The Impossible Dream' had been realised: Watford were preparing for top-flight football for the first time in the club's 101-year existence.

Taylor gave his squad the best possible preparation, taking them away to a remote hotel in Norway. The four games scheduled were incidental and the fact that Norway was basking in the hottest summer since the turn of the century did not disrupt Taylor's plans.

'Boy, did he work us. We ran from the hotel to the training ground in the morning, ran back, then ran again to training and back. Then we would have a game in the evening to play. On the other days, he organised a third session. It was the hardest pre-season training we had ever experienced.' Bolton shakes his head, glad that particular aspect of the game is behind him.

Taylor would later argue: 'If nothing else, we made the First Division fitter.' Certainly there was no squad fitter than Watford's.

'In some way, playing in the top flight was sometimes easier than playing teams from the Fourth and Third because maybe they are not that used to playing against a high-tempo, physical game. We would test any team's fitness and resolve. You had to come up to the mark if you wanted to beat us and some did.

'A lot of times you can be beaten before you even go out on the pitch. You read these names on the programme, then go out and play against them. It was a case of believing what you see and not being cowed by the names. And the Gaffer had instilled in us that whether we play in front of a small crowd at Hartlepool or at Old Trafford, we stick to what we do and do not let the crowd affect us.'

Watford, in their promotion season from the second tier, had added two special ingredients: Cally and Barnesy.

'I was not surprised when he brought in Cally. Barnesy was easy on the eye and the most technically gifted player I have ever played with. Everything seemed so simple to him. Barnsey was so fit: the club's cross-country champion year after year. I remember him playing for us at QPR and he was surrounded in the corner by three players. It was clear he was going to be kicked into the stands but he dropped a shoulder, shuffled and left them all for dead as he moved down the goal line.

'But I think Cally gets overlooked. He was not as spectacular but Nigel was in there for 90 minutes every game. Like Beckham, he could cross the ball from ridiculous angles and with pinpoint accuracy. Nigel was physically stronger than he seemed.

'I ended up with Nigel as roommates. I never asked: I got him. He would drive me mad, sitting up until four in the morning, pinging his Nintendo or whatever. I would wake up shattered or wake up with his music on. He was a lovely lad – very schoolboyish even as he got older – but I can still hear that game thing going "ning, ning, ning".

'Barnesy and Callaghan had extra qualities and took on defences. It was all about being effective; doing the right things in the right area.'

Bolton remembers it took six or seven games in the top flight to believe they were there by right and to stop showing too much respect: 'We reminded ourselves: we deserve to be here.'

The controversy over 'the Watford way' had been fanned in Division Two, particularly when Taylor was recruited to handle the England Under-21 squad and purists worried about him corrupting the purity of England's youth with 'route one' theories.

'People accused us of being a long-ball team. Did people expect us to compete equally against Liverpool and Man United, with their budgets? Yet we absolutely hammered Arsenal at Highbury and other top-quality teams. We hammered them playing our way,' Bolton argues. 'I respect today's managers Dyche and Howe in that they play to their strengths. They haven't got the budgets of the big teams. You have to cut your cloth.'

Taylor, in a letter to me in the summer of 1982, had predicted the furore, fanned by ex-internationals and some sections of the press.

Says Bolton: 'We definitely had a siege mentality. The men who really got our hackles up were QPR and Terry Venables. We beat them 4-1 in the League Cup and then 4-0 in the League on the way to promotion to Division One. If we beat them we would ask: "What is your explanation now?"

'Leicester, a couple of seasons ago, caught the Premiership out. Teams were unable to believe that they played with such intensity. It was similar with us, and they had various people trotting out excuses, such as John Bond of Manchester City. It all helped to fire us up even more.

'We beat Sunderland 8-0. Their manager admitted their keeper was Man of the Match, which is one hell of a statement. Look at those performances and results over those years. They were not a lucky streak. Those were consistent performances and results while we moved forward. To dismiss Watford as a long-ball team was just a label and did not scratch the surface of what we were all about.

'Jeff Powell of the *Daily Mail* was an advocate of Terry Venables' style. I respect that viewpoint, but he did not add the fact in his criticism that he respected our results and achievements over six or seven years. We were dismissed as worthless, which was silly.'

Bolton recalls opposition forwards asking why they couldn't play the game properly, claiming the ball was just hoofed upfield with no skill involved.

'It was a defensive reaction because they did not have anything else to say because they were being beaten. Let's go back to Liverpool of the 1970s and '80s, and they did not play tippy-tappy football. Some coaches try to make the game so difficult because it suits the way their teams play and conduct themselves. QPR and Tottenham were so cultured that everyone used them as the models to aspire to but we beat them.'

But Bolton remembers when the superior class and football exposed them: 'That ball through from Dalglish and on to Rush at Anfield that season. Dalglish sold me totally. That haunts me to this day. I did actually clap him for that. I had to go "wow".

'I had trouble mastering Garry Birtles of Forest. Not the quickest, not one to mix it with you, but I never got the better of him. But there were so many highlights such as doing the double over Arsenal. It was a magical experience but then the whole era was just that.

'We sat back at the end of that season and we felt we had done a decent job by finishing second to Liverpool. I don't think it sank in so much then. Seriously, to achieve that, I think we were in some sort of bubble. Did you seriously entertain that? Did the Gaffer seriously think six years down the road we would be playing in Europe?

'It was exciting to play throughout those years, but after years of listening to supporters, I know it was exciting to watch. It was consistent entertainment. We had our off-days but one of the greatest tributes to the players and club was that the supporters came and watched, even when we struggled a bit. As the Gaffer said: "Give me 100 per cent: that is what I expect. I can't, and supporters won't, accept anything less than 100 per cent."'

Bolton would find himself playing in Sofia the next season in the UEFA Cup – a long way from those fraught, early days of his career. 'I remember they really hacked at us, and me and Wilf said: "OK, that's how it goes then." We hacked them down in turn and got away with it.

'Imagine that, playing in Europe just six years after we opened at Stockport in Division Four. It was amazing.'

Watford had upset many purists, but their all-action, forward-thinking, high-pressure game had stunned the First Division in their first season in the top flight. But not all of their opponents were critical.

'I remember when we lost in the League Cup 7-3 at Forest in 1982. We came into the dressing room and sat down. The door is flung open and in comes one of the greatest managers of all time: Brian Clough.

'He looks at us: "You lot: I f***ing love you." Then he turned and walked out.

Graham watched him go and then said to us: "Do I need to say more?"'

On the Rocks

The fact Bolton's marriage was in serious difficulties was one thing, but to have the details printed in the local newspaper was something else. Graham Taylor stressed the need for Bolton to 'sort out his marital problems for once and for all, and get back to form'. He also stated the centre-half would not be considered until these problems had been resolved.

'It was a bad period but I understood he was supporting me in a way,' says Bolton. 'He was informing the fans that my form had dipped as a result of domestic problems.'

In retrospect, Bolton says he held on to his deteriorating marriage too long, instead of grasping the nettle and informing his wife that enough was enough as others, including Taylor, would have done.

'It was a time when I made some bad decisions,' he admits. 'My head was in a whirl. I was getting on the coach to go to

Prague in the UEFA Cup second leg, when the Gaffer comes to me and says he has received an offer from Brentford, which was acceptable. I promptly asked him if I was in the team but when told I was on the bench, I decided to stay behind and talk to Brentford. It was the worst football decision I ever made.'

The £5,000 deal was accepted by the manager in December 1983 because he despaired of his charge ever putting his problems to bed.

'Brentford offered me a better deal financially than I had at Watford. They were struggling in Division Three. Why did I go? Good question. I, along with my wife Chris, were part of the Watford scene, part of the club. I thought perhaps if I changed clubs, the marriage would get back on track,' he reflects. 'I was grabbing at straws really.

'I had two years left on my Watford contract but Brentford offered me a two-year deal. It was the worst decision I ever made. My marriage broke up two months later, which I was unable to stop. Furthermore, the fire had gone from my game. There was no passion in my play. I was spent whereas I think if I had remained at Watford, I would have got my form back. My marriage would still have floundered but I would have been in the right, supportive environment to get over that and get back my enthusiasm for the game. Who knows what would have happened? With the injuries they had, I might well have got back into the team and played in the FA Cup final the following May.'

It is a view shared by his second wife, Tina, who contends that if the couple had got together a year or two earlier, Bolton would have remained a successful and hungry Watford player for at least a couple of seasons. Instead, 31-year-old Bolton stood at the top of Clarendon Road with Luther Blissett one Sunday May morning, cheering and waving at their former colleagues, as the losing FA Cup finalists took a bow during the course of an open-top bus tour of the town.

Luther was less than pleased with his fortunes after leaving Vicarage Road, as was Bolton. I remember seeing them standing and waving, and I felt sad on what was otherwise a happy day, for I knew they both wished they had stayed at Watford, for what Graham Taylor later described as the peak of the upward climb.

'Yes, had I stayed at Watford and played in the FA Cup final, that in a sense would have completed the journey,' says Bolton. 'There is a trapdoor at the end of your playing career. You are earning relatively good money and are generally well thought of. I was getting £350 a week with £250 a point. But that trapdoor is there. In a sense, towards the end of your career, you are standing on it and no one prepares you for it opening.'

The Brentford experience did not go well. The manager who bought him, Fred Callaghan, made way a few weeks later to be replaced by Bolton's boyhood hero, Frank McLintock, who he had watched from the terraces at Filbert Street. McLintock had been among those who had been critical of the so-called 'Watford way' and he did not rate Bolton's contribution.

'Frank was a lovely man and we got on well. But I was not for him or his style of play. So they offered to pay me up at the end of the season and I agreed.'

The trapdoor opened and Ian Bolton went out of League football, just six months after being pencilled in as substitute for Watford in Europe. He was sent tumbling down the ladder to non-League Barnet, and even that appointment was due in part to Taylor pulling the strings with the Underhill boss, Barry Fry.

'I was training Tuesday and Thursday evenings and playing for the first team, while I worked as a car salesman for Ford in Enfield, with a friend who was sales manager. I was earning £92.50 a week plus commission and playing football for Barnet for a few hours. Then I was made redundant after nine months, unemployed for three and the next thing I knew was that I was working on a building site as assistant site-manager. That was a wake-up call: on site at 6:30 a.m., mixing and carrying cement and sweeping up. I did that for a year.'

While at Barnet, Bolton read Jimmy Greaves' autobiography detailing his heady career and descent into alcoholism. 'He ended up at Barnet too and it was a timely read for me. The realisation came that no one is going to pay Ian Bolton big money for doing a job.

'At Watford, players were not allowed to develop outside businesses. It is understandable really. If you have problems with the business or concerns, it will detract from your football performances. Look what happened to me when I had the marital problems. But the fact is you are molly-coddled as a footballer. Everything is done for you. Then you fall through that trapdoor and you come face to face with real, everyday life. You come out of the football world – that bubble – and face realities such as income and council tax: things you never had to consider. The club did all that. There ought to have been something to prepare you – guidance or a course in what happens when you hang up your boots. When I look back, it took me four years to get football out of my system. I had no other skills.'

His football career took in Kettering, where 'my football passion began to come back', and then on to Kingsbury and Hayes, 'where I really enjoyed playing again', and Chalfont. But by then Bolton was approaching 35, injuries had taken their toll and he needed longer to recover from them, so eventually he decided to call it a day. Even so, he counts his blessings for he has long since appreciated that – had his first marriage limped on – he would have moved back up north and 'I don't know if I would have survived.'

Yet he did survive and prosper and that was down to two people. The first was Tina whose brother, Bob Brooker, played for Brentford with Bolton.

'He had made his debut for Brentford against Watford and I had kicked him all over the park. He said introducing me to Tina was his revenge,' he smiles.

In fact some might have thought Bolton was courting potential disaster for, within four months of his first wife moving out, Bolton and fellow divorcée Tina set up home together. On the face of it, it was a rapid romance with the possibility of them both being on the rebound. Thirty-three years later the couple are still together, proud parents of daughter Carley and granddaughters Ruby and Pearl – 'my precious gems'.

'Actually Tina was at the same stage in life that I was,' he says, reflecting warmly on the days when he found he was no longer alone and regurgitating them in a series of soundbites. 'She had got divorced. Tina was so grounded. She was already a bank manager when I met her. She was earning more than me. I was so lucky to have met her. She stuck with me through those ups and downs.'

Bolton worked in the club shop at Oxford United while they won the League Cup, and then found his post-football niche and forte as a salesman: 'I really enjoy the work and meeting people.'

The first stint as a salesman was for a Bedford company and he was soon promoted to head salesman. Subsequently he applied for a job at Watford firm Sara, who specialised in industrial garage doors and loading-bay equipment. It was then he met the second post-football mentor.

'Graham was the big influence when I was playing football, taking over from my dad. But then I went for an interview for a post as European sales manager. I did not think I had much hope of getting the job but I was interviewed by the boss, Andrew Cannon. What a man. He saved my life in many ways.

'He is a kind, generous and honest man – so similar to GT. I became his number two and had ten glorious years before he sold the firm. After that I moved to Milton Keynes and then back to Sara. I am still a salesman and enjoying life.'

He keeps in touch with Andrew Cannon and likewise did so with Graham Taylor until the latter's untimely death. 'I was so pleased I kept in touch with Graham and Watford, where I played a part in co-hosting on matchdays. I love the Watford association because it was the most important part of my football life.'

He has only put on a few pounds since his playing days. 'I am lucky in that in close season I would go on holiday to the States, fully indulge and come back for pre-season two or three pounds lighter. Whereas Simsy could lock himself in an iron cage all summer and still come back overweight. In those days the Gaffer would fine you if you put on weight during the close season. You had to look after yourself.'

In keeping with many ex-professionals, Bolton finds it frustrating watching the modern game.

'I have become a little disillusioned with football in general over the last few years. I know you have to move with the times but I think the supporters pay a vast amount of money to watch their teams, and I am sitting there after 70 minutes, counting four shots on target, seeing tippy-tappy, sideways, backwards football and I am not being entertained. In Graham's day as long as we scored one more goal than the opposition, that was what was all-important.

'When I was playing, nine out of ten clubs were owned by local businessmen. It was typically a local man owning a club. Now, it is all about the money and big business. There is not one ounce of romance or sentimentality.

'Yet, put yourself in the position of every chairman running a club: they are running a business. There was not the money sloshing around in my day. Now it is unbelievable and unimaginable. Imagine: managers are two games from getting the sack. With the Pozzos and Abramovich, everything is justifiable if they are to achieve what they want to achieve. At the end of the day they are running a business; it is all about the bottom line. Football is becoming more and more corporate and going away from the grassroots. Will it continue with all this money or, as I sometimes fear, one day will it all go pop?'

Plainly unrepentant, he scoffs at the ancient and erroneous nickname 'Mr Long Ball'.

'Ask the fans if they were bored or entertained,' he argues and with undoubted merit. 'That climb from Division Four to Europe and the Cup final is well known as an amazing football achievement, but what is missed is that we did that together. It was not just the players, manager, Elton and the staff, but the entire community. We were truly all in that together with the fans. That is what makes that achievement so much more exceptional and so memorable. The fans were with us all the way.

'I personally think what GT did could be replicated one day. That's not to detract from what he and we did. You need a chairman to back you and stand by you. It is down to the manager to get the right players to adopt his pattern of play. Getting from the fourth tier to the second would be feasible. The hardest is getting from the Championship to the top flight, but with a set game-plan and players convinced as to its worth, it could be done again,' he contends.

I thought back to my earlier interview with Ross Jenkins in his Spanish garden and his fond remembrance of a shout that echoed down the pitch for a number of years, for Bolton's concept of reviving the style of Watford's play from yesterday would need certain qualities if replicated today. Even 37 years later, when watching Watford or anyone on television, as the ball is played sideways and backwards, I still yearn to hear the occasional shout: 'Get on the end of this one, Ross,' and seeing that amazing, accurate ball with its arrow-like trajectory drop some 50 yards upfield onto the big man's chest.

Those indeed were the days. That indeed was one hell of a player: a true Watford legend.

3

LUTHER BLISSETT

BY MIKE WALTERS

A Star is Born

Once upon a lifetime, football was not a competition to see who could spend the most money or who could sustain the largest debt beyond third-world banana republics.

As Britain emerged from the power cuts and three-day week of Edward Heath's government in the 1970s, there were no orchestrated protests on social media if clubs did not throw at least £150 million at new signings in a single transfer window to placate entitled fans struggling to reconcile ambition with solvency. There were no oligarchs, oil barons or captains of industry turning the Premier League's top six into a sterile, cynical exercise of privatisation. As one comedian pointed out on Twitter, in 2017 annual spending on defence among global powers read as follows: USA £820 billion, Cuba £700 million, Manchester City £200m, Bosnia £180m, Congo £135m.

In more equitable times, the joy of football was rooted in a sense of communal belonging, where supporters identified with the players who represented them, and the two parties forged a bond which transcended sport. In the most satisfying examples, clubs would nurture talents who became not only the heartbeat of a team but part of an entire town's fabric.

Watford Football Club's rise from the lower divisions was masterminded by Graham Taylor's expertise as a manager and Elton John's safety net as a guarantor at the bank, but they did not simply buy their way up the League. While the hooligan dark ages infested the game elsewhere, Taylor's greatest achievement was to establish Vicarage Road as an oasis of safe, inclusive family entertainment. And on the pitch, his team enjoyed a rapport with fans which went way beyond the bilateral arrangement of money at the turnstiles going directly into players' wage packets. They represented us, we liked the way they represented us, and we adopted them as extended family.

Luther Blissett played more games, and scored more goals, for Watford than anyone in their history, and he became the club's first ambassador to play for England. Yet those facts scarcely begin to explain why his name is synonymous with the Hornets. If the empire Taylor built was a showcase for all that was good about football when most clubs' attendances were falling, Blissett was the missionary who never stopped spreading the gospel.

He may not have been the most naturally gifted player to wear Watford's colours, but he was the most venerated – to the point where his surname became superfluous. With respect to Idris Elba's excellent TV series 30-odd years later, there is only one Luther, just as there is only one Elvis, one Marilyn, one Elton. Even supporters who have never met him have been on first-name terms with Luther since his first appearance on the teamsheet. When he uncorked enviable ability to go with that jaguar pace, he never imposed limits on where his potential might take him. Where that big smile radiated warmth and dignity, we relished Luther's success like gardeners taking pride in their annual crop of tomatoes in the greenhouse.

When nostalgia holds sway and we cast our minds back to how enjoyable football once was – compared with the glorified trade show it is now in danger of becoming – many of the images will feature Blissett rampaging across YouTube footage, a big cat hunting down its prey across the plains. We adopted him, we were proud of him – and even when he left, for Milan or Bournemouth, the prodigal son always returned to his spiritual home. No billionaire or sheikh's bottomless pit of disposable income could ever put a price on the umbilical cord between a legend and his flock.

It is fair to say Blissett was a wild card, not an ace in the pack, when he first appeared on the first-team radar at Vicarage Road. Yet by the time he made his final appearance for Watford 16 years later, he had taken up permanent residence in the hearts and minds of all those who had followed his journey, his irresistible pace and endearing personality straddling the biggest staging posts of the Hornets' history.

Luther was more raw than a steak tartare when Mike Keen handed him his first start, but it was a stunningly prophetic glimpse of the future: 'You always remember the first time you do anything important in your life, and as a footballer that means your debut and your first goal. I believe I managed to score on my home debut everywhere I played, but of course my first goal in senior football was special because I had just turned 18 and it's always important for a young striker to break his duck, to experience that euphoria and want more of it.'

On the Easter weekend of 1976, Watford played three games in four days – consecutive home matches with Torquay and Swansea in the space of 24 hours before a bank-holiday Monday trip to Exeter. Just imagine the squealing and posturing from Premier League managers now if they were confronted with such a breathless schedule.

Unsurprisingly, after the goalless draw with Torquay on Good Friday, not all 5,436 patrons returned to Vicarage Road for a second helping on the Saturday afternoon. But the 900 who stayed away missed a seminal moment in Watford's history – the day a star was born.

'I'd been scoring goals for the youth team, scoring goals for the reserves and I'd come off the bench in a couple of home games earlier in the season, but Swansea was my first start,' says Blissett. 'To tell the truth, I was disappointed that I had not been involved a lot more, and a lot sooner, because Watford had sold Billy Jennings to West Ham for £110,000 the previous year, which was a lot of money at the time. But if I'd kicked up a fuss, I was concerned that I'd be cast as a sulker or troublemaker, and that would only have set my career back further.

'We were in the Fourth Division for a reason, so we weren't a great side. I didn't play very well personally, and I don't think the game itself was much to write home about, but I remember how the goal went in: my back to goal, edge of the box, feint to go down the line, roll the defender with my first touch, rising shot with my second, back of the net. It was one of those instinctive things that you did, especially as a kid, because nobody has told you to do anything different. That's why young players always bring such a breath of fresh air to a team – they have no fear, their verve is based more on instinct than formula, and they have a sense of invincibility. It's a gift you can't teach young kids, but you can probably coach it out of them.'

Born in Jamaica, Blissett had arrived in England as a five-year-old. His father was a carpenter and his mother worked as a cleaner and at the McVitie's biscuit factory in Harlesden. Like any household, there were rules and he was expected to abide by them, but he was afforded the freedom to play football outside until 10 p.m. in the summer. Luther's love of the game was rooted in the best breeding ground of all – the street – and, inevitably, it spread into the grassroots at junior level.

He says: 'I played for Kingfisher Youth on Sundays, and we used to come up against Ryder Brent Valley, which was Cyrille Regis's team. From back to front, they were basically the Middlesex age-group county side. They had all the best players in north-west London, and even as a schoolboy Cyrille was already an absolute monster. They battered everyone except us – they would still beat us by two or three clear goals whenever we played them, but at least we gave them a contest.

'Even at that level, you developed an appreciation of the game. Having started out as a left-back in junior football, then as a centre-half and left-wing, you get a feel for what players don't like. When I was a full-back, I didn't enjoy it when a winger ran at me and got behind me because defending when you are facing your own goal is harder than dealing with opponents who are in front of you. So when I became a forward, I understood that getting beyond the last defender, into the space behind him, was the best spot of all, like landing on Mayfair when you play Monopoly. People used to ask me why I wasn't such a big fan of ball-to-feet . . . Why get the ball played to feet, with a marker snapping at your ankles, when I'm going to get there first 9.5 times out of 10 if you play it into the space behind him?'

Blissett's grand entrance – scoring in a 2-1 win against Swansea on his full debut – was not a false dawn, but the sunrise was still a long time in coming. His next start would be another 13 months in the pipeline, for the last game of the season at home to Darlington. Manager Keen had been sacked, leaving behind a prototype list of players he had earmarked for release on free transfers – which included Blissett.

Sometimes a change of leadership can work wonders for a player's confidence and release their potential like the mayor of Munich's ceremonial untapping of the first barrel at the Oktoberfest. Graham Taylor's arrival at Vicarage Road gave Blissett's career a new lease of life, and three goals in his first five appearances of the 1977-78 campaign suggested he was finding his way. Blissett's favourable impression on GT included a late winner against Darlington that he couldn't even remember after an earlier collision had left him feeling groggy. His late arrival at the far post to sink the Quakers was a welcome antidote to the shock of on-loan striker Bobby Svarc being carried off just 37 minutes into his debut with a knee injury so serious that he never played professional football again.

That season, Blissett's most memorable contribution was not among the six goals he managed in 17 starts, but one that got away: a late, acrobatic bicycle kick against the underside of the bar at West Bromwich Albion in the League Cup, where the Hornets took an accomplished and full-strength First Division side down to the wire before going down 1-0. But the bright light that flickered would burst into flame at the start of the following campaign, when Watford trailed Newcastle United – newly relegated from the top flight – in the League Cup second round at the interval. Jim Pearson's header still separated the teams when Blissett was summoned from the bench, and he regards the 25 minutes which followed as the launch-pad for his career.

'I must have spent 85 or 90 per cent of the Fourth Division title-winning season as substitute,' he says. 'But Graham was building his team, he had brought in the likes of Sam Ellis, Dennis Booth and Ian Bolton, and I was still learning my trade. I still felt very much like part of the set-up, and I was happy to bide my time until the opportunity came – and that Newcastle cup tie was the perfect showcase. We're a goal down, and I've got nothing to lose when the Gaffer sends me on with the message, "Go on, son, show us what you can do." It was the perfect script.'

If scoring against Swansea on his full debut two years earlier was a young striker coming of age in football terms, Blissett's two-goal winning hand to sink Newcastle was arguably his graduation. If the equaliser was a controlled, first-time finish at the far post – with less composure, it was the sort of chance which could have threatened the bulbs on Watford's new scoreboard at the Vicarage Road end – the winner, as the ball sat up invitingly, six yards out, was not his cleanest contact. But who cares?

He recalls: 'I was not overawed by the opposition. I didn't sit on the bench thinking, "Wow, Newcastle, big club, famous black-and-white stripes." I was never blinded by reputations; I didn't care who was on the other side. My only intention was to influence the game and make a difference to all my team-mates. It never bothered me that the Newcastle of old was built around legends of the game because that had no bearing on the Newcastle I was facing that night. The players who made that club what it was weren't around any more. I was blessed with the naïvety of youth, if you like, and it paid off.'

Pride goes before a fall, as the saying goes, and before the week was out Blissett's scoring streak would continue but he would be introduced to one of the harsh realities of Taylor's regime. Four days later, the Hornets went to Gillingham for a Third Division game featured on BBC's *Match of the Day*. In a topsy-turvy 3-2 win, Watford's man of the moment scored one, made the opener for Roger Joslyn, and finished considerably lighter in the pocket.

Joslyn was a rugged competitor who would later haul Watford over the line by their bootstraps when their promotion campaign was running out of steam. Blissett recognised the value of Joslyn chugging through midfield relentlessly where others became bogged down in mudflats, quicksand or snowdrifts. 'It was horses for courses – what Roger could do, I couldn't do. Later in that season, he dragged us through a rough patch where things weren't happening for us because he only knew one way to play: all or nothing. He put his heart and soul into it – you never needed to go looking for him, and he scored twice at Gillingham, but I learned a costly lesson that day.

'The ball has gone out of play and the linesman's had a shocker. It was obviously our throw-in, no guesswork required, and he's given it the other way. I told him what I thought and the referee has booked me for dissent. Fair enough, if you allow too much backchat, you get anarchy. After the game, Graham Taylor pulled me aside and said, "Listen, you've had a good week, but you'll be of no use to me if you're sat in the stands serving a suspension later this season. One thing I won't tolerate is my players being booked for dissent." He fined me a week's wages, and I was never booked for dissent again in my career.'

While Luther learned the value of keeping his thoughts to himself when officials were mistaken, you cannot put a price on the events which launched him into uncharted orbits of celebrity a month later, when Watford were handed a slingshot and took down one of English football's giants.

The League Cup third-round draw sent Taylor's buccaneers to Manchester United, the team Blissett had supported as a boy. Little did we know there would be so many viable contenders to follow, but if the clocks had stopped around 9:30 p.m. on 4 October 1978, the Hornets' 2-1 win would have been arguably the greatest result in the club's history. Only the FA Cup quarter-final win against Liverpool eight years earlier could have rivalled it and, like that famous afternoon when the Liver bird's wings were clipped, Watford's highlights reel was burnished with flying headers.

Chairman Elton John had grasped the sense of occasion by flying up to Manchester in a private jet, with Taylor's wife Rita and their two young daughters among the VIP passengers, and Watford rewarded their day-trippers with an assertive performance, much as they had taken the game to West Brom and West Ham on cup assignments the previous season.

'We had fallen behind, despite giving at least as good as we got and having the better chances,' recalls Blissett. 'And once we had equalised straight after half-time, we played with a belief and conviction that made people watching the highlights on *Sportsnight* think, "Wow, who are these guys? Are they really in the Third Division?'"

Word had spread that the BBC's midweek showcase for live sport, where boxing title fights or cup ties were invariably top of the bill, would feature the Hornets' trip to Old Trafford as the main course. In those days, top-flight clubs did not treat the League Cup as an inconvenience and fleece supporters by fielding second-string teams. Cup shocks were not a rite of passage for lower-division sides, and there was a greater sense of adventure about the competition. Many young Watford fans who had been unable to make the midweek trip to Manchester in term-time tuned in without knowing the score and woke up the entire neighbourhood when Blissett met Bobby Downes' driven left-wing cross with a fine header.

Seconds earlier, Blissett had been chasing down Arthur Albiston's sliced back-pass, which had brought United goalkeeper Paddy Roche rushing out of his 18-yard area, and the immediate danger appeared to have passed when Gordon McQueen's hurried clearance – with his feet dangerously high – cleared the box. But Downes always possessed an enviable ability to deliver crosses at pace, more a five iron than a pitching wedge, and when he wrong-footed Albiston, jinking back onto his right foot, it earned him a yard of space to whip his centre towards the penalty spot before Steve Coppell, funnelling back to help his full-back, could cut it out. Blissett, losing United substitute David McCreery, who had been marshalling him on the edge of the box, launched himself at it. And although Roche, diving to his left, managed to get a hand to it, the sheer pace of the header took it into the corner. Whether you were in the away fans' terrace at the North end of Old Trafford or leaping off the sofa at home, the bedlam was as joyous as it was unconfined.

The evening was only going to get even sweeter. Ross Jenkins, turning sharply, spooned a chance narrowly over the top as the Hornets remained true to Taylor's principle that attack was their best form of defence. Then Watford crossed the threshold between a magnificent performance and an almighty cup shock – and Blissett crossed the frontier between promising striker and household name.

Several tabloid back-page headlines the next morning screamed the same line: SHEER BLISS! Watford's winner, 19 minutes from time, catapulted Blissett towards national celebrity. Some of us even kept a photograph of it on our living-room walls until we got married at the age of 29. There was almost a poetic quality about Blissett's soaring header to make it 2-1, a perfect symbiosis of prodigious leap and execution of finish. The moment it nestled in the bottom corner, teachers all over Watford knew nobody would be paying a blind bit of notice to their counsel at school the following day. Education was suspended – Luther was the talk of the town.

Before sealing their finest upset since that FA Cup eclipse of Liverpool in 1970, Watford had to survive some hairy moments – Jimmy Greenhoff turning sharply and hitting the post, Alan Garner heading off the line from McCreery and, unforgettably, Andy Rankin's impossible save which left United defender Gordon McQueen on his knees, beating the turf in disbelief. But there was an aesthetic quality about Blissett's winner which made it such a worthy contender for the pantheon of Watford's greatest goals.

Brian Pollard, breaking down the right flank, slipped the ball towards Jenkins, whose run towards the corner flag took the towering McQueen with him, leaving ample space in United's box. 'It was textbook stuff,' says Blissett. 'When Ross made that run and held the ball up in the corner, he took two defenders with him – and now they were lying so deep that they could not get back out again to catch us offside if we attacked the 18-yard area. Our right-back, John Stirk, had got forward in support, which was his job when we had the ball, so Ross lays it back to Stirky and then Dennis Booth is waiting for it ten yards in from the touchline.

'As soon as Boothy receives it, I know he's going to cross it and I know exactly where he's going to put it – almost to the nearest square yard. He doesn't need a second look because he knows I'll be on my way to attack the cross before it's even left his foot. The two defenders on the far post [Albiston and Martin Buchan] have got to jump for the ball from a standing start, but I'm attacking it. There's only one winner – they could have been seven feet tall but I'm favourite all the way. I know that if I get a firm contact on my header, I'm going to score. You can see what's going to happen a split second before it actually unfolds. When you hear psychologists talking about "visualisation", that goal was a prime example.

'Anticipation is such a big part of a striker's make-up. When the penalty box is packed, there is an art to making runs to a specific area and knowing the ball is going to reach you. People sometimes asked me, "How the hell did you know when a cross was coming to you in an area the size of a phone box?" and I would tell them we practised those moves so often that I was dreaming about them last night.

'In terms of scoring goals, football is about exploiting time and space. That winner at Old Trafford was created by Ross making his run, taking Manchester United defenders with him and creating space in the box for me to attack. There was no blinding science behind it, but we made it happen. When I watch games now and it's tactical, cagey, the forwards are static and there's no movement up front, I want to pull my boots on again. Too many statues. Get on your bike, make something happen.

'Where does that night at Old Trafford rank? Right up there. It was special because United was the club I had supported as a kid, idolising George Best, and it was easily the biggest crowd I had ever played in front of, the biggest stadium I had ever played in, the biggest single result of my career up to that point. I was having the time of my life.'

England Calling

Those two headers at Manchester United made the world sit bolt upright.

Down the years, English football has been littered with broken dreams or kids who got too big for their boots before they had even learned how to tie their laces, and Luther Blissett's profile after felling one of the game's giants spiked like a must-have commodity's share price on the stock market or an electrocardiogram registering a heartbeat. But instead of the latest Ranger Rover or overpriced watch, Luther brought only a level head and a manager with the wisdom of Solomon to the party.

'Being decent in the air, and scoring with my head, was always an important part of my game, although it had never come to the fore until I scored those two goals at Old Trafford,' says Blissett. Among the 28 goals with which he decorated his 'eureka' season, there were plenty more from the land of nod. There was a pair of headers to sink promotion rivals Swindon, a mid-air collision with Exeter goalkeeper Vince O'Keefe where sheer willpower held sway, and the opening goal in the League Cup semi-final first leg against reigning champions Nottingham Forest, with the England goalkeeper rooted to the spot in the City Ground mud.

Headers make headlines, and on the perfect evening when the Hornets clinched promotion to the second tier with a 4-0 win against Hull, the carnival was already in full swing by the time Blissett completed the scoring with a perfunctory dip of his brow. It was only his second goal in 12 games – perhaps a signpost towards leaner times ahead – and although he began the following season up front, for a couple of years his goalscoring feats reached a plateau. There was a stellar, two-goal performance in a home win against West Ham – a game notable for the violent infiltration of East End charmers at the Vicarage Road end – and a fabulous, rasping finish in the shock 3-0 win at Wolves in the FA Cup. But if Blissett finished the 1979-80 campaign as the club's leading scorer, he was also becoming more acquainted with the right flank and deeper-lying patrols in midfield.

If he was content to add strings to his bow, the arrivals of Malcolm Poskett – a clinical finisher, if not much more – and Gerry Armstrong appeared to block Luther's route back to the front line until he finished the 1980-81 campaign with three consecutive winners. The first, squeezed in from an unlikely angle at Meadow Lane on a filthy Easter Saturday, forced Notts County to put their promotion champagne on ice; the second, with time almost up at Vicarage Road, thwarted Sheffield Wednesday; and on the bank-holiday Monday at Wrexham, Blissett's late strike ultimately delivered a top-half finish and gave Graham Taylor the feeling that Watford were ready to 'make another move' the following season.

Blissett, too, sensed it was time to ruffle more feathers among Second Division defenders. To score 23 goals in a season which culminated in the Hornets' elevation to an unprecedented orbit was commendable in its own right; but considering his first goals of the season did not even arrive until mid-October in the 2-1 win at Cambridge United, it was an impressive return by any yardstick. In fact, Luther scored 17 of those 23 goals after January 26, carrying his prolific form into Watford's historic maiden voyage in the top flight.

Like goalkeeper Steve Sherwood, there is a compelling case to argue that the calendar year 1982 represented the zenith of Blissett's career, the best football of his life. The 20-year-old who stunned Manchester United had matured into a dynamic, consistent goalscorer with a more complete understanding of his beat. And when he veered into the frame for an England call-up that year, it felt like a triumph of pure sport. No big-club favouritism. No teacher's pets promoted ahead of more gifted pupils.

This was an England international, made in Watford. The first man in the club's 101-year history to make the grade. And he did it without barking profanities at referees or feigning injury. He did it without slapping in transfer requests when he was dropped or demanding pay rises he hadn't earned or rising to the bait in the face of unspeakable racist abuse. Everything Luther achieved on a football pitch was down to his spirit, appetite for hard work and never taking his athleticism for granted.

The enchanted journey from the Fourth Division was simply fantastic, but somehow it felt validated by Blissett's England recognition. Like getting your passport stamped, a phenomenon with which he was about to become regularly acquainted.

'Playing for your country is something every player wants to do, but it never really crossed my mind that I would go on to represent England,' says Luther. 'They had Kevin Keegan, Trevor Francis, Tony Woodcock and Paul Mariner – I didn't spend my time worrying about England because I couldn't see how I was going to be picked ahead of players of that quality. There was no need to put added pressure on myself because it never seemed a realistic prospect in the first place.

'My job was to score goals for Watford, and that was my only concern. I hate it when I hear managers say that it doesn't matter who scores the goals as long as you win the game. When you're a striker, it *does* matter. That's your job, it's what you're paid to do.

'As far as I was concerned, there was a pecking order and if it was going to happen, it would happen. What I would say is that in the early weeks of our first season in the First Division, I was probably on top of my game more than at any stage of my career. I wouldn't say I felt invincible, but I had scored twice against West Brom to put us top of the League [although it was only five games into the League season] and the four against Sunderland came in our next home game. I'd hit the ground running, which was pleasing because I hadn't played at First Division level before, but I still didn't think international recognition would come my way. You have to earn England caps – you don't just hit a purple patch for a couple of weeks and expect the phone to ring.

'It's not right when players have one or two good games and think they should be playing for England when that's not necessarily the case. A rush of goals should bring you to the attention of the England manager, but it shouldn't automatically mean you get in the squad. And it's never easy to walk into a squad where a nucleus have been part of it for three or four years, especially if you don't play for one of the "big" clubs. To feel comfortable, you have to be there by right and mixing with people who had to work as hard as you to reach that level. It's no different to being an apprentice who has to learn the trade at his club and earn the right to be part of the first-team squad. I don't think enough young players go through that process any more, where they polish the senior professionals' boots, sweep the corridors and clean the toilets. By the time I was called up by England, I had scored goals in all four divisions, played for the Under-21s and appeared for Watford in midfield, out wide and as a central striker.'

Was playing for England everything Blissett hoped it would be? It was his misfortune to enter the gladiators' arena during a dip in the national team's fortunes as they missed out on qualification for the 1984 European Championship finals in France. But it was still a moment of unsurpassed parochial pride for Watford supporters when Luther the First stepped off the bench for his debut on 13 October 1982.

'It was everything I dreamed of, and expected, up until we played the actual games,' he says. 'It's all brilliant when you get called up and you are not just representing your country but your family, all your relatives and the people who have helped you along the way. Then there is all the interest from the newspapers, TV and radio, who want to interview the new kid on the block, and that's all good because it's part of the show.

'Before kick-off, there was a difference between winning my first cap against West Germany at Wembley and my first start against Luxembourg a couple of months later. I was on the bench against the Germans, so you didn't walk out of the tunnel with the team – you followed on behind and made your way around the dog track. When I was in the starting XI, and you walked across the pitch, you knew there were a few people in the crowd who had always given me abuse when I was playing for Watford – and for all I knew, there were probably still a few doing so that night. But I can tell you, when you wear that white shirt for the first time and you think of all the people you are representing, it's one day in your life you will never forget. Ever. Then the whistle goes, and it's another football match. For me, the best part was everything leading up to the game because once you were on the pitch, the mechanics of your job were the same as club football.'

The distant hum on Fleet Street's grapevine that Blissett was nearing England service became a cacophony when he finally scored his first hat-trick in senior football, more than six years after his Watford debut, in the 8-0 annihilation of Sunderland in September 1982. On 19 previous occasions, Luther had found the target twice without turning it into a treble, but this time he was simply unstoppable. As a performance, it followed the template for relentless, attacking football that Taylor had set two years earlier in the Hornets' League Cup miracle against Southampton – where Blissett had played wide on the right and was not among the scorers in an extraordinary seven-goal trashing of the odds.

Blissett's four-goal haul against the shellshocked Mackems included the goal which embodied everything Taylor stood for: direct, simple, thrilling football. Ian Bolton's raking pass down the line, Nigel Callaghan's perfect, first-time cross and Luther's leap to meet it with an emphatic header was stunning in its execution. Four goals to the good, Taylor had told his team not to sit down in the dressing room during the interval because he wanted them to maintain the momentum of a destructive first half where they could have fallen behind before Sunderland walked into the path of a whirlwind.

'The Boss told us to keep moving, to run on the spot and keep our muscles "awake" because he didn't want the second half to become an anti-climax,' says Blissett. 'I reaped the benefit more than anyone, and my second goal [to make it 5-0 and open the floodgates again in the second period] was one of my favourites in a Watford shirt. People who dismissed us as a kick-and-rush side should watch the video of that move and apologise. There wasn't a speck of hit and hope about it. If Glenn Hoddle had hit that 50-yard pass like Webby, everyone would have been raving about it. Cally didn't even need to break stride or take a touch before sending over his cross – which was inch-perfect, by the way.'

Interviewed for ITV's *Big Match* that night, clutching his first match ball as a trophy, Blissett looked vaguely surprised when he was asked about the possibility of an England call and almost heroically steered clear of tub-thumping: 'That would be nice, wouldn't it?'

The summons duly landed within a week. For his first home game in charge, against the beaten World Cup finalists, Bobby Robson was still dealing with the fall-out from his decision to omit Kevin Keegan – who was not amused to learn of his exclusion via the media rather than a personal phone call from the manager – and Luther was among the wave of new recruits drafted in.

Blissett says: 'It was almost like the changing of the guard, time to move into a new era. That was probably the right game for Bobby Robson to look at new players, to find out which ones were prepared to poke their heads above the parapet, so none of that stuff ever affected me. The only person who could shape my future as an England player, when I walked out onto that pitch, was me. It's what I could do that mattered, not debates about other people and whether they should have been picked.'

Blissett's debut amounted to nine minutes. He was sent on in a triple substitution, as England trailed 2-0 to a pair of Karl-Heinz Rummenigge goals, and made his presence felt in a late rally, although Robson's side ultimately fell short despite Tony Woodcock's reply five minutes before the end. But Luther's finest hour in an England shirt came two months later: a hat-trick on his full debut, in the 9-0 flagellation of Luxembourg at Wembley, which remains England's biggest winning margin for more than half a century.

Say what you like about Luxembourg – at times, they defended with the aptitude of a pub team and made a mockery

of the adage about no easy games in international football –
but this was another lightbulb moment for Luther.

All three goals involved Woodcock in the build-up. His first,
a tap-in, rolled over the line apologetically after the Arsenal
striker's shot had been blocked by overworked keeper Jeannot
Moes. So eager had Luther been to devour the rebound and
complete the formality of opening his England account, that he
shanked it. The second was an instinctive header as Woodcock's
powerful shot from a tight angle ricocheted back off the bar,
and a diving header, unmarked from five yards out, was a lovely
way to bring up his hat-trick: pick your spot, pick that one out.

'The two headers were all about getting yourself in the right
place, and anticipating where the ball was going to drop. The
first was not the cleanest contact, to say the least, but it was still
the most satisfying. Like my first goal for Watford, I'll never
forget my first one for England. Maybe it didn't look as pretty
as the other two, but it was just as important.'

They proved to be Luther's last goals among his 14 England
caps, although he remained part of the squad until 1984. His
last appearance came in a friendly 2-0 defeat by the Soviet
Union at Wembley – a fortnight after Watford's FA Cup final
appearance where, much like England's fruitless toiling against
the Russians, he was a helpless bystander.

Before the curtain fell on Blissett's international ambitions,
however, there were some memorable contributions – notably
an energetic display in the 3-0 win against Hungary in Budapest's
Nep stadium, and a 13-minute cameo against Denmark which
came agonisingly close to transforming a moribund England
performance. Trailing 1-0 to Allan Simonsen's penalty, Luther
was denied a stoppage-time equaliser when he swivelled to
meet a half-chance from Kenny Sansom's long throw, only for
Danish keeper Ole Kjær to make a brilliant save. 'If anything,

I almost caught it too sweetly – it might well have gone in if I'd mishit it,' reflects Blissett with a rueful smile.

Earlier in the summer of 1983, Watford had performed their own celebration of London buses: you wait 100 years for the club to produce an England international, and then two come along almost at once. When Blissett was hooked in Belfast, during a stodgy 0-0 draw with Northern Ireland, his replacement was none other than 18-year-old Hornets team-mate John Barnes.

They would play together, for little more than 20 minutes, against Australia in Melbourne the following month before Blissett addressed another important landmark in his career on the national team's return home: his million-pound transfer to AC Milan. But there was a feeling, prevalent among Watford supporters, that Barnes and Blissett were wasted by England like a pair of greyhounds in a tortoise derby. That view was not spawned by any superiority complex, but after the high-tempo thrills of the Hornets' hammer-and-tongs approach, international football was a pedestrian spectacle. Watford chairman Elton John, among others, despaired of the strolling tedium.

'In the end, you're almost that square peg going into a round hole,' confides Blissett. 'You would probably have needed another three or four Watford players on that pitch for us to make the impact we had been making at club level. The players we had at Watford were not suited to slow, keep-ball, possession football – our strength was getting at the opposition, going for the jugular, but England didn't often play that way. When we did go for it – like the game against Luxembourg – it was a more "English" style of play and we destroyed them. But more often that not, the tempo was much slower.

'For me, we were falling between two stools – we weren't good enough to play keep-ball, and we weren't good enough to change gear suddenly because it was often safety-first. For instance, when I played against Hungary at Wembley, I was instructed to mark Tibor Nyilasi, who was a decent playmaker if you let him get on the ball up in dangerous areas. My job was to stop him from playing and get forward to help Trevor Francis when I could.

'I know Bobby Robson spoke to Graham about it, because he knew I had done a few shifts in midfield for Watford, but I have always been of the view that if a manager asks you to do something for the team, you do it. That's your job.'

Luther can recall other moments where he could have scored, or should have added to his three goals for England, but he has no need to reproach himself. The privilege of making the grade and earning his 14 appearances will forever outweigh what else he might have achieved. He was the standard-bearer for Watford in a golden age for the club in terms of international recognition.

Barnes, who won 31 of his 79 caps as a Watford player, was a prominent victim of England's ponderous approach. If you didn't scream at the TV when Barnes was forced to leave the handbrake on and 'drop in' when full-back Kenny Sansom went charging into space better suited to an out-and-out winger's exploration, the nurse will remove your gag and masking tape now.

Ben Foster, a Manchester United player who spent two years on loan at Watford, won his first senior cap on the back of his exemplary form in 2007, and he remains the only other player to appear for England as one of our own at Vicarage Road. From the Rocket Men era, Gerry Armstrong scored a famous winner for Northern Ireland against hosts Spain in the 1982 World Cup finals when he was a Hornet. And Kenny Jackett won 31 caps for Wales – the first of them three weeks before Blissett's England debut. 'He was so unlucky,' says Luther. 'If his career had not been curtailed by injury, Kenny could have won two or three times that number. And he was so versatile, he could have won them anywhere on the left side of the pitch.'

Was Blissett's international career unfulfilled, then? Nothing will diminish the pride of Watford supporters in his achievements, but the favourite son himself admits: 'My one disappointment is that I never got to play in a World Cup qualifier leading up to the 1986 finals in Mexico. But, hey, if the manager didn't think I was good enough, perhaps I was better off out of it.'

Milan

Among the 19,318 spectators at Watford's thrilling, last-gasp win against Aston Villa in February 1983 was a scout from Italian giants AC Milan.

The Rossoneri were looking to sign a prolific goalscorer as a talisman of their resurrection after a troubled period in which they were relegated from Serie A following their implication in the so-called Totonero match-fixing affair. And they were prepared to spend £1 million to get their man. In an age when Premier League clubs are awash with TV money, £1 million is barely loose change from the petty-cash tin or a month's wages for a headline act, but by 1983 only a handful of players – Trevor Francis, Clive Allen, Steve Daley, Andy Gray and Bryan Robson – had been bought for seven-figure sums by English clubs. By any yardstick, £1 million was a king's ransom.

According to the apocryphal version, Milan president Giuseppe Farina ordered his spy to run the rule over 'Watford's outstanding black player' – and instead of returning to the San Siro with a glowing dossier about John Barnes, who had a rare off-day against Villa, the scout allegedly went home raving about Luther Blissett. As well as being offensive in concept, the story does little justice to the professionalism of a major power broker in the European transfer market. How could a huge club like Milan go shopping for an exotic winger with a limbo dancer's elasticity and end up bidding for a fast, direct, out-and-out goalscorer? The very idea is patently ludicrous.

Yet, when uncorroborated rumours surfaced in Italy that Milan had suffered crossed wires and effectively confused Barnes and Blissett at an identity parade, that did not stop certain elements of Fleet Street picking it up and running with the story. Luther has the broadest sense of humour imaginable, but he has never seen the funny side of that tale.

'It was, and is, very disappointing that one or two newspapers printed the story because it's a racist thing to write,' he said. 'To say Milan made a mistake because there were two black players on the same side and they got them mixed up is racist. And secondly, Milan had told the world they were looking for a goalscorer – so are they going to come after a guy who scored 33 goals in all competitions that season, more than any other striker in Europe, or his team-mate who was a wonderful player but scored 13? With respect, I don't see how they could possibly have made that mistake. We were completely different types of player. If they wanted me to score a hatful in Italian football, maybe they should have signed both me and Barnesy. At least he would have played to my strengths.'

Watford had suffered two heavy defeats at Villa Park – a comprehensive 3-0 loss in the League and a 4-1 reverse in the FA Cup fifth round – when the European Cup holders came calling at Vicarage Road. In the cup tie, a week earlier, the Hornets had been thwarted by a combination of impatient finishing, inspired goalkeeping and improbable luck. This time, they went ahead early when Blissett's emphatic finish grazed the underside of the bar, and they looked like being forced to settle for a point after Mark Walters' freakish equaliser until Wilf Rostron's skimming-stone winner in added time.

Milan's watching representative would have been enthralled by the entertainment and, for the record, Blissett's performance on the day was a perfect example of his talents: always a threat, he scored one goal, hit the bar with a superb, cushioned header and he was a menace throughout. He had endured a few taunts about his finishing, including the cheap-shot adjustment of his surname to 'Luther Miss-it' in some quarters, and one critic even tried to sustain the 'joke' by claiming Blissett nearly missed the target when he scored because his shot had shaved the woodwork on its thunderous flight path beyond Villa keeper Nigel Spink. What a clown.

Sure enough, Milan made their move at the end of the season. Taylor, in no hurry to dispose of his leading goalscorer, tried to frighten them off by quoting a million-pound asking price. Just as chairman Elton John did not blink when GT warned him it would cost a million to take Watford from the Fourth Division into Europe at their first meeting in 1977, Farina was not going to let a mere fortune prevent the Rossoneri from landing their prime target. A week later, he matched Taylor's valuation. Now it was down to the player himself to decide whether to stick or twist.

The Hornets had just returned from a groundbreaking trip to the Far East, where Blissett scored twice in a 5-1 win against the Chinese national XI at the People's Stadium in Peking (now Beijing), and his off-season was further curtailed by England's tour of Australia. In the final instalment of the trilogy, a 1-1 draw in Melbourne's Olympic Park when Barnes and Blissett played those last 22 minutes of the game together – the only instance of two Watford players appearing in the same England team – it would be Luther's last outing before he swapped English football's blood and thunder for *la dolce vita*.

'I had just won the Golden Boot, not only as the top scorer in England but in the whole of Europe,' says Blissett. 'If I was ever going to leave Watford for a move abroad, it felt like the right time to do it. To be honest, there was only a handful of clubs where I would have even considered going – Barcelona, Real Madrid, Bayern Munich, Milan, the usual suspects – and although it felt like the right time to go, it wasn't an easy decision.'

To a large extent, Blissett would be venturing into the unknown because few British players had tried their luck in Italian football. John Charles had been revered at Juventus after joining the Old Lady for a then-British-record transfer fee of £65,000 from Leeds in 1957. The 'Gentle Giant' was top scorer in Serie A with 28 goals and brought the Scudetto title to Turin for only the third time in the post-war era. Trevor Francis had joined Sampdoria, but neither Joe Jordan nor Jimmy Greaves – who scored nine goals in 12 games – lasted more than a year at Milan. Greaves had been reluctant to leave London in the first place and tried to abort his move from Chelsea, but Rossoneri coach Giuseppi Viani refused to cancel his £140-a-week contract.

Blissett and Watford had invested so much in each other's fortunes, so much emotional baggage, that he agonised over the move for hours. Finally, late at night, he picked up the phone and told Taylor: 'I don't want to leave but I would never forgive myself if I passed up this opportunity and I never got another chance like it.' Taylor, pastoral as ever in his duty of care to a valued employee, calmly told his striker that if he wanted to leave, he would go with the club's best wishes – and if he wanted to stay, the club would be happy to harvest his next crop of goals.

'That was a huge relief because it meant there was no pressure, and no hard feelings, whatever I decided to do,' says Blissett. 'Basically, the Boss was saying, "It's your call and I'll back you to the hilt whether you're staying or leaving." After everything Graham Taylor had done for me, I didn't want to let him down or leave him in the lurch. That late-night call put my mind at rest. At the time Milan made their bid, everything told me I should go for it, and now I had a licence to go with my gut instinct.'

At 25, Blissett was in no rush to pack his bags and make a run for it to Heathrow airport, but he was gasping for air after the first meeting between Milan's delegation and Watford at the Hilton hotel on the A41. It was the hottest day of the year, and the three-hour meeting in a small conference room with no air conditioning turned into a survival of the fittest in a sauna.

'It was horrendously hot in there,' says Blissett. 'I was in a suit, and after we shook hands to say hello, I never said another word until we got up to shake hands and say goodbye. It was mainly agents talking back and forth across the table while I sat there like a tennis umpire watching a long rally. It was all very amicable, and when we emerged the Italians said they would report back to the club president, relay to him that everything was in order, and we would meet up again the following week.'

Famously, the deal to take Blissett from Vicarage Road to the San Siro was concluded among racks of suits and overcoats in the basement of a Savile Row tailor. The masonic secrecy would have been hilarious if the sums of money involved were not so mind-boggling for a club of Watford's stature at the time. Graham Taylor, Elton John, chief executive Eddie Plumley and agent Jon Holmes were all on parade with Blissett as they were ushered into the cellar, where they were confronted by a scene conforming to every movie stereotype.

'To be honest, I think the Milan president just wanted to meet Elton,' says Blissett. 'We walked into this tailor and we were escorted down a flight of stairs, through racks of coats and jackets on hangers, into a little office at the back – and there he was, the president himself, sat down with his overcoat draped over his shoulder, flanked by his henchmen. If they had been carrying violin cases, it would have been like a scene from a Mafia movie. It was one of those surreal moments in your life when you think, "Am I on a Hollywood film set here?" But we all got on well enough, and the deal was done in no time.'

Blissett and Taylor embraced like a father waving his son off to university, knowing the nest would never be quite the same without him, and after a memorable season on the pitch, Watford added another record to the slate: for the most expensive player sold, by far, in the club's history.

When he was unveiled at the Stadio Giuseppe Meazza, Blissett admired the soaring tribunes and gasped: 'Blimey, it's a bit different to Watford. Where's the dog track?' And in five pre-season games for his new club, the Englishman abroad scored nine goals. He settled well into his new environment, the only lifestyle drawback a shortage of his favourite cereal: 'No matter how much money you have here, you can't seem to get Rice Krispies,' Blissett once mused.

But when the Serie A season started, the promise of that pre-season goal rush soon proved to be misleading. Where Luther had been feasting on a stream of crosses into the box at Watford, or chasing balls into the channels to test his markers' appetite for a gallop, he was forced to feed on scraps in Milan.

It dawned on him that he was taking on a very different football culture when Milan crashed 4-0 at Avellino in their opening league fixture. 'The change was just chalk and cheese,' he says. 'I had been really looking forward to Serie A after doing well in those pre-season games. I had some very good players around me and I thought they would play me in when I made my runs – but often the ball never came. We just played keep-ball for the whole match and it was very difficult.

'The one thing that annoys me about my time in Italy is when they call me a failure or a flop,' he says. 'To me, a failure is someone who has not achieved anything, or who does not even try. But I played 30 league games that season for Milan – more than anybody else, so I can't have been tripping over my bootlaces every week. And in those days, nobody in Serie A scored 30 goals in a season. Most teams played with a sweeper system and their mindset was, "We've started out with a draw and we're keeping the draw." That year, Michel Platini was the top scorer with 20, Zico got 19 for Udinese and nobody else got more than 14. I scored six goals and was called a flop, but I think our rivals Inter Milan's top scorer, Alessandro Altobelli, scored ten that season – so he hardly filled his boots, and yet nobody called him a failure.

'Platini had the advantage of playing for Juventus, who were the champions, and he took all their penalties and free-kicks. Milan had just come up from the second tier and we only finished three points off a place in Europe. We weren't a million miles away. It sticks in my craw when the media here throw around cheap slogans about "failure" for what I did, when the experience of going to Italy, and everything around it, was fantastic. The preparation, the culture, the religion of football were all amazing.

'The games were shit because if you missed a chance, it would be half an hour before the next one came along if you were lucky. Like Formula One, when technical things become the most important aspect, you can't watch it for too long because it just becomes boring. When you allow the players to express themselves, to get on and do what they do best, football is far more entertaining. But when you are hostage to tactics, shape, discipline and technical smallprint, you never lose the shackles. It's just boring.

'That's not in any way a comment on my team-mates or their ability: Believe me, we had some decent players in that group. Franco Baresi was only 22 or 23 when I played with him at Milan, but you could tell he was going to be a serious defender. And a couple of years later, Paolo Maldini broke through into the first team and they forged one of the greatest partnerships in central defence of all time. I would never disown the shirt because it was a privilege to go through that experience at a great, great club – and the fans never forget the players who get to wear the shirt. You go to Real Madrid, Barcelona, Liverpool, Manchester United, Arsenal . . . the players who represent those clubs are always welcomed back like one of the family. They are never forgotten, always celebrated. It's never about how much a club paid for you.

'But I can't believe the figures knocking around in the transfer market today – bang-average players going for £20 million, and I mean ordinary, run-of-the-mill players. If you apply figures from today's market to the time when Milan signed me, what would it cost to buy the top goalscorer in Europe's major leagues in 2017? You are probably talking £120 million and, I'm sorry, that is outrageous. It is absolute nonsense. You can build a hospital, and pay the doctors and nurses, with that kind of money. Football is losing all sense in the value of money – there is no value. It's like the Italian lire used to be. There are so many noughts on the end of every figure, they have no meaning.

'Too many football clubs are living way beyond their means and it cannot last. Watford were in trouble when ITV Digital collapsed in 2002, and they have recovered well because when you look at the ground now it bears no relation to the old main stand being closed down, falling into disrepair and finally being knocked down. But if the market crashes again, it will take more than collection buckets to stop some clubs going under.'

Blissett's impact on the pitch for Milan may have been limited by the impoverished ambition of tactics around him, but he left an amusing legacy beyond football – among an Italian anarchist cult. A group of activists who claimed responsibility for a series of hoaxes and pranks called themselves the Luther Blissett Project. The group's stunts were nearer university rag week than urban terrorism, and Blissett accepted the notoriety as harmless fun, observing: 'They say all publicity is good publicity!'

He was soon making headlines again on familiar territory though. For, if Watford banked a breathtaking sum when they sold Blissett, gratifyingly they got the same player – weighing in with 20-plus goals a season – when he was repatriated at Vicarage Road 12 months later for barely half as much. The £550,000 Taylor paid to bring the prodigal son home stood for almost 20 years as the club's highest fee paid for a player, and it was a bargain. Not until Icelandic warrior Heidar Helguson arrived from Norwegian club Lillestrøm in January 2000 for £1.5 million did the Hornets spend as much on a signing as the fee they had received for Luther in 1983.

Blissett did not expect to walk straight back into the side, but in any event he did not have to wait long for the picture to become clearer. Although Taylor valued Mo Johnston's predatory finishing, the manager's patience had been wearing thin with the trimmings of his celebrity lifestyle, and when Celtic offered £400,000 – double the amount Watford had paid Partick Thistle 11 months earlier – it was a good deal for all parties.

'When I came back to Watford, I wasn't an automatic choice because George Reilly and Mo had been so prolific,' recalls Blissett. 'And before I could get back in the swing and earn the shirt again, it took ages for the international clearance to come through. The deal was all done, signed and sealed, but I was in limbo for a week because we had to wait for a few bits of paperwork. It would have breached transfer rules if I had started training with Watford before everything had been processed, so for several days I found myself going on long runs through Cassiobury Park and doing a few training drills on my own.

'I wasn't expecting banners, party streamers and a big welcome-home reception, but it wasn't quite the triumphant

return I had imagined. And when I finally got the green light
to join up with the squad, it was a bit strange at first because
I was back at the same club but with a lot of different players.
Ross Jenkins had gone, Gerry Armstrong had left, Pat Rice had
returned to Arsenal, Ian Bolton had joined Brentford, Steve
Sims had signed for Notts County, and a lot of young players
had come into the side.

'Although I had only been away a year, it took me a while
to get used to it. The club itself was much as I remembered it,
and Graham was still running it in much the same way, but the
personnel were very different. I knew the Boss wasn't going to
drop Reilly or Johnston just to put me back in the team out of
sentiment, but that wasn't a problem for me. I had never been
afraid of hard work, or rising to a challenge, going back to the
days when I was looking to break into the first team and had
Ross, Keith Mercer and Alan Mayes for competition. Sooner
or later, I was sure my chance would come and I would take
it. As it happens, Graham put me straight in the team for the
opening game of the season at Manchester United. Although
we didn't quite fire on all cylinders up front, the team played
really well and I had Nigel Callaghan in a friendly headlock after
he equalised in injury time.

'People often ask me whether I got better service from Cally
or John Barnes on the wings. They both had fantastic ability,
but in Cally's case I'm not sure he really understood how good
a player he was. When John beat his full-back, he was gone.
See you later. Once he had beaten his man, you didn't get the
ball back because he left you for dead. Cally would sometimes
beat his man once and then turn back to try and beat him
again – and when wingers fall into the trap of trying to be too
elaborate, that's when they can come up short. But don't get
me wrong, Nigel was a fantastic crosser of the ball, both from
open play and set-piece delivery.'

Favourite Son

After his first season in charge at Vicarage Road, Graham Taylor said he would happily pay good money just to watch Luther Blissett run. By the time Blissett had been catapulted into the headlines, and his double act with Ross Jenkins had sustained Watford's fantasy run from English football's fourth tier to the top flight, Taylor had changed his tune. He would now happily pay to watch him play as well.

There was always a ripple of excitement – if a game was in the balance and Blissett was the Hornets' nuclear deterrent in reserve – when he rose from the bench and went through the gears along the touchline in his tracksuit. Taylor had a point: Luther could move like a panther. There was almost an Olympic sprinter's rhythm about Blissett in full flight.

'Every game I played, whether I was in the starting XI or coming off the bench, I always wanted to receive my first pass in the channels or over the top,' he says. 'I didn't want ball-to-feet – I wanted to find out if the defender marking me fancied a gallop, and to see how quick he was. More to the point, I wanted them to know how quick I was, because that meant you could get inside their heads straight away. I wanted to let the other fella know he was in for a hard time trying to keep up with me. I wanted to lay down a marker and let him know he could not expect an easy time grazing at the back. If the ball came down the channel, I was going to chase it. If the defender got there first – and not all of them did – they all found out I was going to hassle them, harass them and work my socks off to win it back.

'I was lucky to be playing with such a talented, honest bunch of lads that we became friends for life. Every day was a new adventure. All the players who arrived at the club over the years became your mates. We were all in it together – we all lived it, breathed it and enjoyed it as a band of brothers. And, of course, we all owe so much to the man who put it all together and created that harmony.'

When managers weigh up a player's attributes, they look for the three As: Athleticism, Application, Ability. Blissett possessed all three in abundance. The first two were never in question and the third was a matter of transferring the stack of goals he had plundered at every level since his conversion from a left-back, and then centre-half, with Kingfisher Youth to senior football. Before he uncorked that potential, learning his craft in the reserves and on the fringes of the first team, one coach had reckoned Blissett was a creature of hibernation and only liked to play with the sun on his back.

Taylor would expose the lazy stereotyping in his first season. During a cold snap in January 1978, to widespread astonishment, the pitch for Watford's game at York was passed fit, even though conditions were nearer a polar cap than playable. But Taylor had watched Blissett train outstandingly on the ice during the week, and backed his intuition by omitting Jenkins and handing Luther his first League start for 11 weeks. Blissett skated around Bootham Crescent as if he was auditioning for reality-TV show *Dancing On Ice*, scoring once and helping Alan Mayes to plunder a hat-trick in a thumping 4-0 win. He was back on the bench a week later, without complaint, when the big freeze had thawed into mudlarks and the Hornets steamrollered Doncaster Rovers 6-0 at Vicarage Road. The following season, during another harsh winter, Blissett would go through a purple patch of scoring nine times in five games, including two on a snowbound pitch against Lincoln. These were not the prolific exploits of a striker who only came out to play with the sun on his back. He could turn it on in all conditions.

Coached expertly, and heeding Taylor's special attention to set-pieces and attacking the far post, Blissett contributed the lion's share of his 186 goals for Watford in the Rocket Men era of GT's first decade in charge. Like his club-record haul, Blissett's popularity remains unsurpassed.

'During Watford's first season back in the Premier League, under Quique Sanchez Flores, I was presented with an award after being nominated as the club's favourite son,' he says. 'What I didn't know, until he appeared on the pitch at half-time, was that Graham Taylor would be presenting me with the trophy. That made it extra-special. It was a nice surprise, and it meant even more to receive that award from him – although it should have been me presenting him with the trophy. He is Watford's favourite son. He was the town's brightest star. So many people owe him so much, we would never think of it any other way.

'To me, Graham Taylor always was, and always will be, the Boss. With a capital "B". The first time I met him, in that series of one-to-one chats he had with each player when he first came to Watford, I remember he was sitting at his desk with a piece of paper in front of him. We sat there in silence while he stared at this sheet of paper until, finally, he broke it by saying my full name over and over, rolling it around his tongue like an actor rehearsing his lines, pausing for a few seconds between each time. 'Luther Blissett . . . Luuuther Bliss-ett . . . Luther Loide Blissett . . . With a name like that, son, you're going to have to be a star, aren't you?"

'One of the first things he told me was that the previous manager, Mike Keen, was going to let me go, but Tom Walley – who was still registered as a player at the time, but was now heavily involved in the youth-team set-up – had recommended that I was worth another look, and the Boss told me he was going to give me a chance. I wasn't looking to go anywhere so I'm glad Tom piped up on my behalf – and I'm even more glad the Boss listened to him.

'He was as good as his word. Graham Taylor was not just a decent man – he was fair, a man of integrity. If he thought you were swinging the lead, or going through the motions, he would not be afraid to tell you. But even when he was brutally honest, you always knew he was doing it for the right reasons.

'In the history of football, there can't be many managers who had a whole squad, a whole club, a whole town eating out of the palm of his hand. Bill Shankly was a god at Liverpool, and that's what Graham was at Watford – and always will be. What he achieved, and what it cost the club to achieve it, was absolutely ridiculous. Totally outrageous.

'I had so much respect for the man, and what he did for me, that when I came back to Watford in 1996 and joined the coaching staff under him, I still called him "Boss" even then. People asked why I didn't call him "Graham" or "GT" – but I simply couldn't do it. He was always "Boss" to me. Always will be.

'There are certain people you look up to and you put them on a pedestal. When Graham told you to jump, 99.9 per cent of people would jump because they had so much respect for him – and the other 0.1 per cent soon realised they were out of step with everyone else if they didn't. He had that effect on his players – they listened to him because he listened to them. He was a very good listener. If you poured your heart out to him, he would take it all in. It was his way of getting to know you as a person, what made you tick.

'He would also listen to the way you said things because that helped him to weigh up your character. That was his way of doing things, and he was absolutely brilliant at it. Look at the players he bought for Watford in those first ten years: there was hardly a single dud among them because he did his homework on potential signings and he already knew about their personalities before they even sat down to discuss transfer fees or contract terms.

When he scouted new players personally, he used to go and stand incognito on the terraces and watch them.

'Of course, he wanted to find out if they could make a contribution on the pitch and fit in with the way we played as a team. But he attached even more importance to their characters and whether they were compatible with the inner soul of Watford as a club. Later, when I was part of his coaching staff, he would tell me nine out of ten signings don't work out. It didn't look that way to me – as far as I could make out, he had much a better strike rate than that.'

If Blissett has one regret about his association with Watford, which spans virtually his entire adult life, he would concede that it pains him never to have been given the chance to manage them. He gained his first coaching badges as a 17-year-old, to give himself the best possible chance of being equipped to jump on the merry-go-round when his playing days wound down. It is a triumph only of narrow minds that nobody has offered him an opportunity to manage in English football's top seven tiers.

More often than he can remember, Blissett would apply for jobs at League clubs and receive replies thanking him for his interest, but citing a lack of experience as the reason he had missed the cut. He wonders, with some justification, how much experience in football management the signatories of those letters had. 'How many games had they played? I have played in all four divisions, in different countries, and when someone tells me I don't have the experience it is an insult,' he told the *Daily Mail* in 2013.

Regrettably, Watford are among the clubs who denied Blissett an opportunity to sprinkle his stardust as a manager when there was a vacancy and he offered his services. He was not even afforded the courtesy of an interview when

Ray Lewington was sacked in 2005 and the unheralded Aidy Boothroyd was appointed as his successor.

There is no guarantee that Blissett would have been as successful in the dugout as he was on the pitch. Up the road, over the county border, a certain club installed Ricky Hill and later Mick Harford – both tremendous players, adored by the fans – as manager, although one was appointed with the team in manifest decline and the other suffered relegation from the Football League after the preposterous handicap of a 30-point penalty. Whether their unfulfilling stints in charge diminished Hill and Harford's stature as legends in Bedfordshire is a moot point. At least they were given an opportunity.

'I'm not bitter. Everything happens for a reason in football, even if you might not agree with the reasons,' says Blissett. 'I was more than happy to be an assistant manager, working with Kenny Jackett and Graham Taylor. As long as I was playing a part in building something, and hopefully bringing a bit of success to the club where I started my career and had my happiest years as a player, it would have been brilliant. I would have been totally content with that.

'But once Graham Taylor retired, I knew I was never going to get a job at Watford as part of the staff serving under a head coach. Without spreading it too thick, as a long-serving player who always had a great rapport with the fans, I would have been perceived as a threat to a manager. Look at all the people who have had the job at Watford since the Boss – who was going to employ me as a coach? It was never going to happen. There's a saying that you should never appoint a No.2 who could do the job as well as you, if not better, because sooner or later he might get a chance to prove it.

'But I could never understand why managers seemed to look at it from a negative standpoint. I felt I had more to offer than just a connection with the supporters. Would I have been a successful League manager in my own right? We've never found out. As things stand, the only club I have managed, where I have been in charge of running the show, is Chesham United. It's not for me to say whether I got a fair crack of the whip, I just let the facts speak for themselves. But going back a few years, after Graham had retired as a manager, I was taken on as an assistant coach at York. We were flying, at the top of the table, when I was made redundant in the November of that season. They fell away virtually from the day I left.

'Rightly or wrongly, people tend to stick with what they know. Jobs for the boys. That's the way it's always been. A lot of clubs are now based on a business model or a policy of hiring known quantities and – come hell, wind or high water – that's the way they are going to do it. At bigger clubs, they can probably afford to do that because if a section of the fans don't like it, there will always be another 10,000 people on the waiting list for season tickets.

'At clubs like Watford, it's a bit different because every single person who comes to support the team is a valuable member of the club. It's important that the team projects a sense of togetherness, a communal bond with the fans. That's what made Graham Taylor so special: he came in, galvanised the team and took the whole town with him. But at times during last season under Walter Mazzarri, you could see there was something missing. The connection between the fans and the manager wasn't there.

'When we went up to Liverpool and got smashed 6-1, I could tell it was coming. Something wasn't quite right about the chemistry, and it could easily have been double figures. Our two best players were the goalkeepers – Heurelho Gomes, before he went off injured, and Costel Pantilimon. They saved us from total annihilation. In all the games I played under Graham, that simply didn't happen. Sure, there were games when we got turned over, but we never went through the motions and the Boss never gave the opposition a free hit with his body language. He didn't sit in the dugout with his head in his hands, throw his arms in the air or pick arguments with the officials. If you send out negative vibes, you get negative results.'

Mazzarri's departure in May 2017 had not looked inevitable when the Hornets reached the sacred 40-point safety mark with six games to spare. But that lack of being on the same wavelength as the fans, and his conspicuous failure – or refusal – to speak English would lead rapidly to his downfall. Of all the managers and head coaches at Vicarage Road since Taylor, none remained so distant from the supporters, the polar opposite of the communal spirit GT fostered. Mazzarri was only sat a few yards from season-ticket holders in the Sir Elton John stand on matchdays, but he might as well have been in a dugout on the moon. His reign unravelled so quickly in the closing weeks of the campaign that his departure did not generate a murmur of protest.

Jobs for the boys? In fairness, nobody could accuse Watford of subscribing to that manual since Gino Pozzo bought the club in 2012 from the unlamented Laurence Bassini. In the first five years of Pozzo's reign, the average shelf-life of Hornets managers, from Gianfranco Zola to Mazzarri, was eight and a half months. In that period, Blissett fulfilled peripheral roles from corporate matchday host to announcing the teams over the public-address system before kick-off. If he is to be denied his dream of following the Boss (still with a capital 'B') into the manager's office, perhaps it is time the favourite son's contribution to Watford's history was consecrated in another way, especially as another symbolic measure of his service somehow passed him by. For another anomaly – in the lifelong love affair between Luther Blissett and Watford Football Club – is that he never won the club's Player of the Season award.

Blissett is not the only special player in the club's history to miss out on the end-of-term gong. John Barnes, whose extravagant gifts were evident from the moment most fans first clapped eyes on him, never won it either. When you look at highlights and reviews of each season on YouTube, Barnes was involved in a staggering number of goals, whether scoring them or providing assists when double-marked by defenders struggling to contain a repertoire from the Magic Circle.

But in the season when Watford were the second-best team in the land, Blissett was at the peak of his powers. He scored 33 goals for club and country – and nobody in the top flight of any serious division on an entire continent could match him. If the hardest part of football is putting the ball in the net, as the pundits often inform us, Luther's England call-up that season was no accident, nor a simple case of Three Lions manager Bobby Robson simply backing a form horse on a hot streak.

'Let's be honest – in the year we finished runners-up to Liverpool, I had the season of my life,' said Blissett. 'When you've won the golden boot, you've scored more goals than anybody in Europe's major leagues, you've scored your first hat-trick for your club and you've scored a hat-trick on your first start for England, you can't help thinking: "If I don't win Player of the Season at Watford this year, I'm never going to do it." That's taking nothing away from Wilf Rostron, who won it that year. Wilf was as consistent as the day was long when he switched to left-back. And the supporters are the best judges because they are the ones who pay money at the gate.

'It's never bugged me, and finishing second was far more important than personal recognition, but I have wondered how many goals I would have needed to score that season to swing the vote.

'What I do know is that all those goals, and the partnership with Ross, came about through sheer hard work. At first, I'm not sure if Graham Taylor thought it would work. Ross was no slouch for a player of his height, he was decent on the deck and he had the materials to be a very, very good striker. But the Boss formulated a method to get the best out of a target man and a strike partner who was quick, direct and prepared to run at the opposition all day long.

'If you watch my winner at Old Trafford in the League Cup in 1978, who makes the unselfish run down to the corner flag to hold the ball up for John Stirk, and then Dennis Booth, before the cross arrives for me? That was no accident – we practised that again, again and again on the training pitch. On other occasions, it might have been me making that run and Ross would be the one on the end of the cross. We had a great partnership, and it was based on bloody hard work. I like to think the supporters recognised that element as much as all the goals we scored.'

Somehow, for whatever reasons, Luther Blissett may have missed out on becoming the Hornets' manager. Somehow, despite scoring more goals for the club than anyone in its existence, he was never voted Player of the Season. But sometimes it is better to be remembered fondly – not just for the goals and the sheer effort, but the floodlight-strength smile that came with them – and in that regard, Blissett holds a unique place in Watford's history. Among all the trophies, titles and rewards in football, the favourite son is surely an invincible accolade.

I Hated the Cup Final

Let's cut to the chase, because there is little point in sugar-coating it. For Watford Football Club, reaching the FA Cup final in 1984 may have been an unforgettable sway along English football's most celebrated promenade and a crown jewel in the Hornets' history, but Luther Blissett hated every moment of it.

In the year he spent away from Vicarage Road at AC Milan as the club's first million-pound export, the club's favourite son missed out on Watford's inaugural journey to Wembley and he was among the absent friends toasted on their maiden voyage in Europe.

For all the goals he scored and the mountains he climbed, Blissett never played in a Wembley final and he never played in Europe – a glaring anomaly when he contributed so much to Watford's rise, maintained their prominence on the First Division's upper slopes and turned them into a team to be feared in cup draws either side of his Italian job.

'I know it was a proud achievement for the club, but I absolutely hated that FA Cup final day,' he admits. 'Hated every moment of it. Don't get me wrong, I wanted Watford to win it and 100 per cent of me was willing them to do it. But to be left as a bystander, on the biggest occasion every footballer dreams of being involved in, was hard to take. It broke my heart.

'Whatever people may say about the FA Cup being devalued now – which I don't agree with anyway – if you asked any professional footballer in the country in 1984 which game they wanted to play in for their club, every single one would have wanted to reach that final. The FA Cup is still the greatest knockout competition in football because nearly 800 clubs set out in the qualifying rounds in August. That is the trophy you want to win, that is the trophy you want to take on a lap of honour.

'But there I was at Wembley, along with 35,000 or so other Watford supporters, and I didn't really feel a part of it. I recorded the whole thing – all the build-up, all the pre-match interviews, "Abide With Me", the game, everything – but I never watched it. Destroyed the tape. I know even Graham Taylor couldn't bring himself to watch the game afterwards, and I can understand that, but at least he lived the dream. At least he led his team out at Wembley for the FA Cup final.'

On the day, Blissett was hired by ITV as an expert summariser. Standing on the dog track at the tunnel end, where his adoring flock had turned the terraces into a riot of yellow, red and black, he had to halt his live interview to camera more than once to acknowledge the Watford fans chanting his name with a cheery wave.

In truth, Blissett was not the only absent friend missing from the Hornets' Wembley line-up. In 12 months, the team had undergone a radical facelift, mainly through force of circumstance rather than Taylor's appetite for wholesale changes. Of the back four who had taken the top flight by storm in Watford's first season, ruffling more feathers than Colonel Sanders in a chicken run, only captain Wilf Rostron remained as a first choice – and cruelly, unforgivably, he was suspended for the biggest day of his football life after an undeserved red card in bandit country. Les Taylor and Kenny Jackett were still ferreting for their supper in midfield, and service from the flanks was by now well established, but a new double act had prospered up front. Where Blissett and Ross Jenkins had carried such an irrepressible threat 18 months earlier, George Reilly and Maurice Johnston was the new little-and-large combination making hay.

Both had scored in the epic third-round replay win against the old nemesis, in the fourth round at Charlton and the last 16 against Brighton. And Reilly's flying header had been enough for Watford to edge past plucky Plymouth in the semi-final, although replays of the goal are soiled by the sickening 'monkey' hoots from Argyle primitives which accompanied John Barnes on his rampage down the left flank before his perfect assist.

Years later, working on a building site in 2003, Reilly was attacked by a fellow brickie who felled him with a joist and then bit off part of his ear, sneering: 'Remember Plymouth.' With the possible exception of former world heavyweight champion Mike Tyson chomping on Evander Holyfield's ear, it was one of sport's most outrageous carnivore tales. Reilly's earlobe was saved by doctors with the help of 50 stitches and plastic surgery.

'I'd never have believed anyone could bear a grudge over a game of football played 19 years earlier,' Reilly told the *Daily Mirror* in March 2007. 'But I bear no grudge towards Plymouth just because one of their supporters did something horrific. It was just a totally unprovoked attack by a low-life coward who was high on drugs. What is most annoying is that I'm probably better known now for having part of my ear bitten off than scoring the goal that took Watford to Wembley.'

Reilly and Johnston were well policed by Everton central defenders Kevin Ratcliffe and Derek Mountfield in the Cup final, but they were not the only Watford players who came up short on the day. Blissett suspects the enormity of the occasion may only have hit some of them once the bunting had come down.

'Maurice Johnston was only at Watford for a year, and in that time he scored a lot of goals and forged a terrific partnership with George,' says Luther. 'But for everything he achieved that season, and the part he played in helping the club to reach Wembley, I'm not convinced he realised just how much that game meant. Maybe afterwards, when he saw all the fans turn out in the town centre on the Sunday morning to salute the team, he understood he had been a part of something unique.

'I'm not saying the whole occasion passed him by, but Watford should have won that game. Until Everton scored, against the run of play, we had been the better side. I remember John Barnes getting up to Lee Sinnott's first long throw and not quite getting enough purchase on his header to score, Barnesy having another shot blocked and Les Taylor's rebound being deflected just wide, and Johnston missing out on a half-chance . . . maybe it was only a half-chance, but he had been crucifying them all season.'

Johnston had a goal disallowed later on, but Watford were trailing 2-0 by that stage and there was little conviction about the way they went through the motions of a fightback. The last 40 minutes was a tough watch for Hornets supporters, an anti-climax for neutrals and the sum of all Blissett's fears.

'Would we have won if I had been playing? I couldn't convince myself of that,' he says. 'What I would say is that the old maxim in football was as true then as it is now: you've got to take your chances when you're on top. But I hated that day completely. The worst moment for me was about an hour before kick-off, when I was standing on the dog track, just to the left of the tunnel as you look at the pitch, and the players walked out in their Cup-final suits to look at the pitch. There were my mates, all scrubbed up for their big day out, and I'm thinking to myself, "I'm not a part of it. I can't believe it, I'm not a part of it."

'Without blowing my trumpet, I played as big a part as any player to help Watford through the divisions, finish runners-up in the First Division and qualify for Europe. But I never played in Europe – AC Milan had just come up from Serie B when I joined them, so they were not involved in European football the season I was there – and now I was missing the FA Cup final, a once-in-a-lifetime chance for a lot of players. Look, there's no point in being bitter about it or feeling sorry for myself. It was just not meant to be.'

Around two months before the Cup final, when it was becoming clear that Blissett's sabbatical at the San Siro would be nearer a stopover than an extended lease, rumours had begun to circulate that Watford were interested in buying him back, for around half the fee they had banked when selling him.

In the 1980s, the transfer window was not a one-month trolley dash in January for the benefit of Sky Sports to ramp up the hype, and it remained open in England until the end of March.

'It looked as if I would probably be leaving Italy and it sounded like there was half a chance we could get it done before the transfer window shut,' he says. 'I tried not to build my hopes up, but my understanding at the time was that if I signed at least two weeks before the semi-final, I would have been eligible to play against Plymouth at Villa Park and in the final because I wasn't cup-tied.

'People have since asked me if I had been given a fountain pen and I could scribble my signature on any piece of paper at any time in my life, would I have re-signed for Watford so I could have played in the FA Cup final? It's a hypothetical question because it never came to pass, so the answer is no – because when all is said and done, I could not have turned down the chance to play for Milan.

'Everything happens for a reason, and I went to Italy because Milan made Watford an offer they couldn't refuse. But the fact is that I helped the club get into Europe and never played a part when they got there, and I watched them go all the way to Wembley and I wasn't there with them, at least not on the pitch. Two of the biggest things that have ever happened to the club – and I wasn't there for either of them. Totally gutted.'

Provocation

It was like flicking a switch. One moment Luther Blissett was being serenaded with the sickening monkey hoot, the call to arms for primitives at football matches, and the next it stopped – when he rammed his shot into the top corner to put Watford 2-0 up on the night and 4-1 ahead on aggregate. The perfect retort. Have some of that, you racist bastards.

The Hornets' first assignment of the 1980-81 season was
a two-legged League Cup tie against Millwall. Most supporters
have a clearer recollection of what happened in the next round
because it involved the greatest comeback of all time in cup
football – and hundreds of us sent Southampton manager
Lawrie McMenemy yellow souvenir biros to remind him of it
– but Blissett has not forgotten the prologue on a grey Tuesday
night in Cold Blow Lane. It confirmed the initial impressions
he had formed of the place, because Millwall was where he had
experienced his first overt racism in professional football as a
teenager in Watford's reserve team.

The Den was by no means the only hostile, unforgiving
environment for young black footballers to play in 1980, but
it was a stark reminder that – for all Graham Taylor's work in
providing safe, inclusive family-friendly enclosures at Vicarage
Road – other parts of the country were stuck in the dark ages.

Malcolm Poskett's pair of goals in the first leg had given
Watford a slender advantage to take down the Old Kent Road,
but there had been an unpleasant incident when Millwall
fans infiltrated the home support. And here I have to make
a confession: the second leg was the only football match I
have ever attended wearing shinpads. As a protective measure
it was dafter than a box of frogs, utterly frivolous. But it is a
snapshot of the uneasy atmosphere prevalent at some clubs in
an era when many grounds were antique slums and a half-time
excursion to the toilet was like going for a paddle in the dark.

Racism was not the reason we tiptoed into The Den with
trepidation, and nor was avarice the reason my brother and I
ducked under the turnstiles without paying our entrance money
after we finally located the away fans' turnstiles a couple of
minutes after kick-off. The gateman had already cashed up
his takings for the night and he couldn't be bothered to open

his money box again. Another first: getting into watch Watford for diddly-squat.

Millwall fans did not have a tarnished reputation without good reason. Their hooligan culture had even been set before the nation in a *Panorama* documentary in 1977. But on the night Blissett made the bigots choke on their monkey hoots at The Den, racism was a stark sub-plot to Watford's thoroughly competent performance because the taunts aimed at him were so overtly repugnant. Just about every time he touched the ball, it started. Not just in a pocket behind the goal, and not just a couple of dozen uneducated zealots being courted by the National Front, the separatists who used to prey on young football fans as easy converts. It sounded like hundreds of them were joining in. When Blissett scored that evening, the gods were having their say. It was divine intervention.

He says: 'I wasn't surprised by it because I remembered what it was like playing there for the reserves in the midweek league during my first season at Watford. There was hardly anyone there, apart from a few dockers who had probably just finished their shift and maybe a dozen kids who had obviously bunked off from school. These young truants were banging on the side of the tunnel cage, and some of the things they were coming out with were just mind-blowing. I never knew kids of 12 or 13 years old could be so offensive.

'I got a hard time once in a midweek reserve game at Peterborough, and the other incident which always stayed with me was at Crystal Palace in a game where I scored twice – I think both of them might have been penalties – and I went to take a throw-in just along from the dugouts. Five or six lads, all of them old enough to know better, were calling me every name under the sun, absolute filth. I pointed at them and said, "You lot, come and say that to my face outside after the game."

'We're sat on the bus after a good away win, having a bite to eat before the journey home, and one of the boys shouts across to me, "Hey Luth, look who's walking past the coach – it's those lads you wanted to meet." I put down my food and jumped off, with half a dozen of the players in hot pursuit. They didn't actually get off the coach with me, but they stayed by the door to get a good view as I walked over to the Palace fans and said, "Right, do you want to repeat what you said to me when I was on the pitch and you were on the other side of that barrier?"

'They didn't run away, but they didn't repeat any of it. One of them said, "We were only having a laugh," which almost made it worse. It was the equivalent of hiding behind "banter", which is the modern defence for the indefensible. I told them, "Maybe you'll think more carefully about having a laugh in future." I certainly wasn't laughing because I didn't find it funny. As a player, you had to block all of those things out of your mind and focus on what you were doing. That's why, when I play golf now, if someone apologises for talking while I'm lining up a putt, I always say I didn't hear them because I learned to block out all the background noise as a player. It was only the exceptional incidents, or when people were right in front of you, that you couldn't just ignore the abuse.'

In these more enlightened times, the colour of a footballer's skin or his nationality does not register with the majority of fans. Around 25 per cent of professional playing staff at the 92 League clubs are black, and in the Premier League Watford are among the clubs who have fielded 11 different nationalities in their starting XI.

But in the late 1970s and early 1980s, black players were still a relatively rare sight. It was a big deal when Viv Anderson became the first black player selected by England; it was a big deal when Blissett became the first black player to score for the Three Lions and the colour of his skin was a big deal for headline writers. In England, he was the 'Black Flash' – which was probably intended as a tribute to his pace, although the reference to his colour was unnecessary – and when he played for AC Milan in Italy, he was dubbed 'Il Bombardiere Nero' (the Black Bomber).

Along with Anderson, Cyrille Regis and the late Laurie Cunningham, Blissett was a pioneer for black footballers in an age when extremists viewed them as expedient targets for their prejudice. He was not just the heartbeat of Watford Football Club's magic-carpet ride from the lower divisions to the penthouse. Like Regis, who was sent a bullet in the post before making his England debut in 1982, Luther Blissett is one of the most important figures in the game over the last 40 years because he became a standard-bearer for a multi-cultural, inclusive national side. He remains an influential voice for the Kick It Out anti-racism campaign.

And like Regis, his postbag was an unfiltered mix of fan mail and a minority of threats from swivel-eyed pond life who regarded the England team as a closed shop for the far right, not a stage for the best footballers in the land. One letter, shortly after his international debut, warned he would be shot the next time he played for England. Blissett ignored it as the work of a 'crank and a coward'. In these reconstructed times, such unrefined bile would probably have been posted on social media.

'If they were sent anonymously, I never took them seriously,' he says. 'I would have been far more worried if someone had put their name and address on a letter carrying threats because then you might think, "This person doesn't give a shit." They are the dangerous ones.'

Blissett was perceived, in the national media, as a father figure and counsellor to other black players in the Hornets squad. Apart from the prodigiously talented John Barnes, Luther's team-mates at Watford included young winger Worrell Sterling and striker Keith Cassells, whose first team opportunities at Vicarage Road were limited before he went on to score 98 goals for Oxford, Southampton, Brentford and Mansfield.

In reality, it more a case of copying what he did rather than listening to what he said. 'Believe it or not, we never even discussed [racism] amongst ourselves. Sure, we were aware of it, and we had our own ways of dealing with it. And the best way to deal with it was to do the best you could on the pitch.

'In 1984, we were drawn away at Leeds in the League Cup, and three of us – me, Barnesy and Worrell – were all playing and getting absolute dog's abuse. One of the things that sticks in my mind from that night, and I can still see it clear as crystal in my mind when I think back, was running behind the goal to retrieve the ball when it's gone out for a corner. I looked up and almost the whole stand, hundreds of them, were giving us Nazi salutes and "Sieg Heil". Barnesy and I threw each other a look, as if to say "What the f*** is going on here?" So you can imagine the satisfaction when we stuffed them 4-0. They weren't so full of it after we had played their team off the park.'

Poetic justice aside, Watford's win at Elland Road also brought some overdue relief to a porous defence. After leaking 31 goals in their first 14 games of the season, 18 of them at home, they finally banked their first clean sheet of the campaign on Halloween. But it remains a remarkable tribute to Blissett's self-control that he never rose to the bait when he was taunted with abuse which went way beyond the pale. Discipline was a keynote of Graham Taylor's culture at Watford; monastic restraint, however, was his striker's personal triumph.

Blissett was only sent off once in his career – for retaliation, under Newcastle defender Kenny Wharton's uncompromising escort, at St James' Park on the opening day of the season in August 1981. Wharton's tackles were brutal enough, as was Luther's punishment for administering unauthorised retribution, but the proverbial walk of shame was traumatic. By the time he reached the away dressing room, sweat was not the only thing drenching his shirt.

Unlike his booking for dissent at Gillingham three years earlier, Blissett was not fined by Taylor for taking the law into his own hands this time – tacit recognition that he had not been afforded adequate protection when Newcastle were earning the right to play, as the euphemism for aggression goes. But the hostility he encountered on his solo retreat, and the anguish he went through in the changing room as the Hornets' ten men clung on to their 1-0 lead, persuaded him that turning the other cheek was the more righteous path in future.

'I played the game fairly – until I had to look after myself by playing the way other people wanted to play it. When I got clattered, I would never let an opponent know I was hurt – even if the pain was killing me. I would be like a swan on the water: outwardly serene, but quietly raging beneath the surface. And if an opponent was out of order, I was prepared to go over the top,' reveals Blissett. 'And I wouldn't think twice about it. Don't break my leg and I won't break yours.

'I began that season in midfield when I got sent off at Newcastle. Cally had scored our first goal of the season, which turned out to be the goal of the season because it was an unbelievable volley. It absolutely flew in. You could tell it was special because the game wasn't on TV but it attracted about 1,500 votes in the goal of the season poll even though there were only six or seven hundred Watford fans there to see it!

'That afternoon I had been caught late several times and the referee had done nothing about it. But every man has his breaking point, and I just reached the stage where I thought enough is enough. It all happened so quick, but Wharton has come steaming in and as I've turned, although the ball was there, I'm thinking, "You're going to go down this time," and I've done him.

'I sat in the dressing room with my head in my hands, listening to the noise of the crowd. I didn't dare to take my kit off or have a shower because I couldn't begin to contemplate what would happen if we ended up losing the game because I got sent off for doing something so stupid. I didn't get fined for it, though. I think the boss saw what had been going on and decided my suspension would be punishment enough.

'People forget that I had played most of the two previous seasons in midfield, and I had done a decent job for the team there. Instead of hanging me out to dry, Graham just said: "You can't do that." No lectures, no bawling me out in front of the other players. And no fine. Once a class act, always a class act.'

Indestructible

On their magical League Cup run in 1978-79, in an act of solidarity with the chairman, Watford players used to play Elton John's greatest hits on the cassette deck of their team coach to away trips.

When the bus pulled up outside the players' entrance, invariably they would have 'Bennie and the Jets' blaring as loud as the sound system would allow. Evidently, Elton's music infiltrated corners of the soul other rock stars couldn't reach – and not just among his employees at Vicarage Road. More than 25 years later, 'Rocket Man' became the track which inspired England's cricketers to Ashes triumph against Australia after almost two decades of one-way traffic.

Although he was never a superstitious player by nature, Luther Blissett noticed that the only occasion when that distinctive chorus about electric boots and mohair suits was not the soundtrack to the Hornets' arrival at their destination was when they pitched up at the City Ground for their semi-final first leg against Nottingham Forest. It was the only game they lost on that run, and Luther has often wondered if it might have been a different story if the tape had not gone missing that night.

The chemistry between Graham Taylor and Elton was more like brothers than manager and owner, but the players usually maintained a certain respect for a man they called 'Mr Chairman' in conversation. 'We weren't starstruck, but you would see him on *Top of the Pops* on a Thursday night and then he's in the directors' box on a Saturday afternoon,' says Blissett. 'He took over the club when I was just breaking through into the first team, and usually we kept it nice and formal.

'I remember him joining in the dressing-room celebrations when we won promotion, and I remember him performing "Candle in the Wind" at Princess Diana's funeral, thinking: "That's the Watford chairman playing to a worldwide audience of billions," and he got a fantastic ovation – from both sets of fans – when we played Wycombe at home the following day. But the best time I can recall with him was on an end-of-season tour of China in 1987. That was a brilliant trip.'

Blissett always breaks into that famous grin when he recalls the day Sir Elton joined his squad in a game of five-a-side, as Watford kept the engine ticking over between games at the Great Wall of China Cup. The Hornets won all four games to lift the trophy after beating the host nation 2-0 in the final, a match watched by an estimated TV audience of 100 million viewers.

Promising young midfielder Tim Sherwood had made the trip, and he would break into the first team as Dave Bassett steered Watford expertly towards the rocks after Taylor's departure for Aston Villa. Observing Taylor's maxim to train as hard as he played, Sherwood did not stand on ceremony if there was a 50-50 tackle to be won . . . even if a superstar was on the receiving end.

'If there was a ball to be won, you won it,' Blissett told the *Daily Mail* in 2016. 'We had this young lad of 18 making his first trip with the first team, and he was desperate to make an impression. I remember someone passing the ball to Elton and Tim sets off, full speed. You're thinking, "Oh no, Tim – slow down. Tim! Tim . . . ?"

'This is all happening in slow motion with the rest of us watching. I will never forget Tim clattering into Elton John and Elton flying up into the air. It took an age for him to come down, and we are all stood there, open-mouthed. Elton, to his credit, gets up, smiles at Tim and on he goes, having the time of his life.'

Blissett, too, was in his element after another decent season yielding 15 goals in 42 appearances. He scored five goals in four games on tour in China – his best purple patch since the back end of Taylor's last notable FA Cup run as a manager in the 1986-87 season, culminating in that stormy quarter-final win against Arsenal at Highbury.

It would be too dismissive of a famous club, with a rich history and grand heritage enshrined in marble halls, to say it was like nicking sweets off kids in the playground – but Arsenal handed over an awful lot of jelly babies and fruit gums to Watford in the Rocket Men era. A stormy Cup tie finished awash with controversy, with Blissett bearing down on a lonely John Lukic and beating him at the second time of asking, while the Gunners performed their familiar line dance with arms in the air, expecting a reprieve from the officials which never materialised.

Luther's first goal to equalise – a superb near-post volley after David Bardsley had skinned Kenny Sansom, not for the last time that afternoon – remains underrated both in the context of the match and its technical execution. 'Yeah, I enjoyed that one,'

Blissett says. 'I always look back on that game with a smile, partly because we beat Arsenal again the following week at home in the League, and I scored in that one as well. But after all the magical nights, cup shocks and one-off occasions turning over the "big" clubs we enjoyed under Graham Taylor, that was to be his last one as Watford manager.'

They say nothing is forever in football, but the bond between Blissett and his mentor remained unbreakable, even when Taylor sought a new challenge with relegated Villa at the end of that season, and Luther had appeared indestructible himself after two major injury setbacks in the space of seven months.

Luther was presented with a macabre souvenir of the night he fractured his skull against Manchester United in May 1985, a sobering footnote to an extraordinary Hornets rampage. Just 48 hours earlier, Watford had slain Tottenham 5-1 at White Hart Lane, with Blissett among the goalscorers. For the sixth consecutive meeting, Watford and Spurs traded wins on each other's turf, but the margin this time was startling and on any other weekend it would have been more prominent in the headlines, but it was overwhelmed on the news agenda by the terrible Bradford fire disaster, where 56 fans perished.

Remarkably, on the following Monday night, Watford repeated the dose against United. Ten goals in 48 hours against two of English football's big guns. Just imagine the back pages, and the hullabaloo on social media, if that happened today. Admittedly, United were five days away from their FA Cup-final date with Everton, and Ron Atkinson's men may have been treading carefully for the most part, but one collision with goalkeeper Gary Bailey brought Blissett's season to an abrupt end: face-down on the Vicarage Road turf, head bleeding. Fractured skull, as it turned out.

'It was all going brilliantly, and I've scored my first goal against United since *that* night at Old Trafford seven years earlier, when I put my head in where it hurts and it meets Bailey's knee. I finished the season next door in Watford General. I can't remember how long I was kept in for observation, but when I came out I bumped into our groundsman, Les Simmons, and the present he gave me still makes me laugh out loud.'

On the final whistle, and since it was the final home game of the season, Simmons had marched over to the spot where Blissett had been lying, poleaxed, after his shuddering encounter with Bailey and cut out a square yard of turf stained with the Watford striker's blood. Simmons, whose long service was sustained by a mischievous sense of humour, presented it to Luther as a memento of the occasion.

'What do you say to a bloke who cuts out a clump of turf with your blood on it and hands it to you when you come out of hospital – except thank you? Even though I probably had a headache at the time, I had to laugh,' says Luther.

There would be a happier reunion with United the following season, when Blissett's campaign was blighted by a four-month lay-off after he fractured his patella against Leicester at Christmas. (Typically, for several minutes he tried to carry on playing with a kneecap that was essentially broken in two.) Restored to fitness just before the end of the season, Blissett marked his comeback with an equaliser against United after Mark Hughes, who was saying his fond farewells after agreeing to join Barcelona, had volleyed the visitors in front at Vicarage Road. It was another reminder of Luther's enduring aerial power, a far-post header to meet Lee Sinnott's cross, followed by a joyous celebration in front of the scoreboard to announce he was back. It was also the eighth time in his career that United keeper Chris Turner had been forced to retrieve the ball from his net at Blissett's expense after seven previous inquests at Sunderland. No goalkeeper was ever troubled more by Luther.

We may have thought Blissett was indestructible, but
sadly the empire Taylor built was not fireproof, bulletproof
or Bassett-proof. When Dave Bassett took over as Watford
manager in the summer of 1987, his errors of judgement
were not just plentiful but fundamental. Mistaking attacking
football for stripped-down directness was one thing; to build
it around Trevor Senior – a prolific marksman for Reading in
the lower divisions but ill-equipped to be the proverbial target
man, was a colossal miscalculation. To identify two-time Player
of the Season Tony Coton as a potential weakness was simply
mind-boggling.

That Blissett finished top scorer in the League, with just
four goals, in the relegation season of 1987-88 speaks volumes
for Bassett's impoverished ideology in his stopover at Watford,
and Steve Harrison was unable to prevent the Hornets' drift
towards the rapids. 'The funniest man I ever came across
in football,' says Luther. 'Steve could have been a stand-up
comedian in his own right.'

Harrison reached the conclusion he was not cut out to be
a manager but better suited to the mechanics of coaching –
and he may have been right – but there was little wrong with
his scouting instincts. Paul Wilkinson, Neil Redfearn and Rick
Holden were all Harrison signings which indicated sound
judgement, but his reign also marked Blissett's second parting
with Watford. Eager to promote younger strikers in the squad,
Harrison allowed his former team-mate to join Bournemouth,
where a promising manager named Harry Redknapp was
making headway on the Dorset coast.

Any pangs of remorse about leaving his spiritual home
evaporated as Blissett scored four on his home debut for the
Cherries against Hull, and in three seasons at Dean Court he
stockpiled 56 League goals, topping Bournemouth's scoring
charts each time. 'Harry got my career going again and I

loved my time down there,' he says. As a young apprentice, Redknapp's son Jamie used to clean Blissett's boots – although he was 'hopeless' and Luther used to end up scrubbing them himself – but he maintains a fondness for the club and the Redknapp dynasty.

He still has an occasional round of golf with Harry, whom he jokingly describes as a bandit on the course, but when Redknapp returned to West Ham and Tony Pulis moved into the manager's office at Bournemouth, Blissett was like a homing pigeon. He found only a shell of the club which had qualified for Europe eight years earlier, and momentarily he had doubts about going back for a third stint as a player at Vicarage Road, but his heart ruled his head: 'I had never thought that it would be great to go back again, but when Tony Pulis wanted to bring in his own players at Bournemouth, the possibility of finishing my career at the club where I had started suddenly came up, and I just had to take that opportunity.'

Blissett's last appearance in yellow at Vicarage Road, in May 1992, brought the favourite son's career neatly to a full stop, signing off for the Hornets with his 186th goal for the club in a 5-2 demolition of Bristol City. All good things come to an end – and some things which deserve a beginning, such as managerial ambitions, never even make it to the starting gate. Approaching his 60th birthday, Luther is just about over the frustration of a mainstream coaching career that didn't happen.

English football is poorer for the waste of his expertise, but the grand old game's loss has been the Bobby Moore Fund for Cancer Research, Men United's prostate cancer fund, Kick It Out and motor racing's gain. As if to reinforce our perception that he is indestructible, Blissett walked away with barely a scratch after rolling his Morgan Roadster in a spectacular crash during a celebrity classic race at Silverstone in 2011, indulging his passion for cars and speed.

His place in Watford Football Club's history looks equally invincible. Favourite sons come along only once in a lifetime, and we will never tire of Luther Blissett's story – because of all the players to represent the Golden Boys, none conveyed more joy to his flock.

4

ROSS JENKINS

BY OLIVER PHILLIPS

Waste of Money

The long blond, flowing locks that gave him the appearance of a Nordic warrior during those good old days have gone. They are now perhaps longer, more silver than grey, and bunched in a ponytail. Not surprisingly, he is more lined with the passing years but he exudes the air of a man who has lived those and subsequent years with great satisfaction.

When Saturday comes or there is a host of matches in mid-week, Ross Jenkins will fold himself into his small family saloon and drive down to his favourite football bar in Javea on the Costa Blanca, Spain – now his home, and previously his refuge since the day he signed for Watford back in November 1972. He tries to keep an open mind when he watches the modern Premier League action but quickly he becomes frustrated. Along with most of his former team-mates from the halcyon Graham Taylor era, he finds much of the modern game tedious.

'A lot of people seem to think there is a formula for football and are searching for it. My view is that people try and make football a complicated game. It is a simple game, made difficult.

'We played attacking football, and we did not pass the ball across the back and then back to the keeper. What would have been the point? The opposition goal is up the other end. Yes, we got some stick but ask the fans if they enjoyed those days.

It is no good looking the part in defence or in midfield if you don't create chances and win games,' he argues.

'We at Watford were getting bad criticism in our day. A lot of managers seemed to be saying what amounted to: "We know how to really play the game but you are more successful at it." They had their agenda.

'The classic answer was Leicester in 2016. They got it forward, after defending a lot more than we did, and won the Premier League by ten points. Every manager would have liked to have been in their shoes. The players were picked and bonded so well and they captured the imagination of the public. Their supporters will never forget and I became a supporter that season, loving their style and commitment. So refreshing to see them thrashing the so-called big boys with direct, cutting displays.

'Chelsea played good, attractive football to win the title under Conte, and so did Spurs at times. But so many teams seem to have this unwritten law that everyone has to touch the ball at least once before it goes over the halfway line. It is passy-passy and very little or no progress. And the whole point of it eludes me. What did David Pleat say at Graham's funeral? If he was a manager now, he would mix it up a bit? There you are: one of our biggest critics has admitted it has gone too far the other way.

'If we had just humped the ball down the field every time we gained possession, it would have been aimless and unattractive. But we did not do that. Now they pass the ball around all the time, as often as not getting nowhere, and that is aimless and unattractive.'

Jenkins defends Watford's Taylor-inspired style of play with great pride and zeal. 'We opened up areas to exploit by moving defenders around and creating space for penetration. Football is about attacking the main danger zones. Why is the ball hit to the back post nowadays when no one is there? Or it is hit short and does not get to the near post because the first defender intervenes? Those two posts and the area around them are the biggest danger zones.

'We were a team of attackers and when we lost the ball we became a team of defenders. The people who called us "route one" were blind. We hit the ball to the flanks and we had someone there or moving there.

'Barcelona get the ball back from the opponents as soon as possible, preferably in the opposition half. That was our maxim. It is called a high-pressing game now. We just believed the opposition were at their most vulnerable if we dispossessed them in their half.

'And why are there so many short corners when the danger areas are the same as they were for 100 years or more – by the posts? If you put it into those areas, the ball might be cleared, but you have a second wave coming in to regain possession and set up a chance.'

Although living hundreds of miles apart, Jenkins and Ian Bolton both remonstrate at the TV screen when they see free-kicks or corners not getting past the first defender. Bolton has likened Jenkins to a Peter Crouch of his day: tall, talented and with an eye for goal but Jenkins wonders who is teaching the modern centre-forwards. He watches Andy Carroll but fumes at the West Ham target man's failure to be in the England team and, in doing so, reveals the thinking in the Taylor days.

'He picks up a lot of injuries by throwing himself into situations he can't win. He has great potential but there are a number of things in his game that need improving. He is static when he does not have the ball and the centre-half is happy because he has him in his sights. Strikers should pose the defender problems by moving out to the wing. Then the defender is unsure if he should follow him or not. Watching Chelsea's Costa, that is what he did – he offered to take the centre-half for a walk and Hazard exploited the space he left in the centre. Space is so hard to find, you have to move around to open up spaces.

'When I think of learning striker-play – whether it was from Ernie Walley at Crystal Palace or Graham at Watford – you had to pose the defence problems by your movement and positioning when you did not have the ball.

'I watched Watford, as always, but they kept passing the ball around the back in 2016-17 as if it was a sparring session. I could go on. Suffice to say the top flight needed us back in the 1980s and they needed Leicester more recently. The Premiership improved the following season thanks to Leicester showing them up. If I see passy-passy in a match, I turn to another screen in the bar. Sometimes when I watch modern football, I get the impression certain players are not fully focused, perhaps wondering if they remembered to book the restaurant for that night.'

* * *

For two or three seasons after Jenkins signed in a Watford club-record deal, some fans would compete in their attempts to be creative in rubbishing the striker. It would be claimed any one of Snow White's seven dwarfs could out-jump him; that he was 6ft 3ins and jumped 5ft 10ins; that he was a puppet with some strings severed or moved like Bambi on ice. The fans were harsh, dismissive and often reached the point of ridicule but they reflected the generally accepted viewpoint that manager George Kirby, once a ferocious goalscoring striker, had 'bought a pup'.

I will not attempt to rewrite history or appear to dilute the terrace admonishments, but I would pose the question: did we have an unfair and unrealistic expectation?

Jenkins had made 15 First Division outings, scored four League goals over two seasons and caught Kirby's eye in a reserve-team fixture when he netted four. These facts pointed to the conclusion that Jenkins was neither a prodigious scorer nor a very experienced League footballer. In transfer terms he constituted a gamble but for Watford to pay a record fee, rising to £35,000, it seemed a desperate gamble. To put the fee in proportion, while accepting rising football fees were in advance of inflation, the £10,000 Watford paid for Cliff Holton in 1958 would have been the equivalent of £17,000 in 1972 when the Hornets splurged out twice that amount on the very inexperienced Jenkins.

So the weight of expectancy was on his shoulders, for he was designated to cure the club's striking ills in the third tier, despite the fact that he had only a fraction better than a one-in-four strike record at Palace. However, he was tall and so Kirby saw something of his own image in him, although the striker would spend 11 years at Vicarage Road being told by successive managers to be more physical but 'would never become the kind of striker who let defenders know I was around'.

All the evidence suggested that this was a long shot for success but such was the publicity and the hype – coupled with the fact that Jenkins' Watford debut coincided with the club's first away win in 18 months – they brought an unrealistic assumption to the entire saga.

Kirby believed a manager's main weapons were 'man-management, some talent and a great dollop of bullshit'. He embraced the latter element and, while stressing Jenkins was also a long-term investment, Kirby was so excited by his capture that he asked me to set up the printing of a board and posters proclaiming the 'Emperor Roscoe'. Fortunately there was some delay in determining who was financing this exercise, by which time the concept died a death of potential embarrassment.

Signed in late November, it would be almost three and a half months before Jenkins scored his first Watford goal – part of a brace in a 5-1 win over Scunthorpe United that was met with some derision and ironic cheers from supporters. Two goals in 29 appearances was a dismal return and appeared to confirm his status as a flop.

'In ten years, he will still be scoring goals,' said Kirby, whose successive purchases, each breaking the transfer record – bringing Duggie Woodfield and then Jenkins to Vicarage Road – played a part in earning him the sack.

'People no doubt remember that time. It was a difficult, unhappy and demoralising time. Everything seemed to be going wrong. You just wished you could disappear for a while,' says Jenkins of that first half-season. Later, in a newspaper interview after having 'turned the corner', he confessed he had contemplated calling it a day on his football aspirations.

What was not known was that his wife Eve had been suffering badly after a major operation and their baby, Ross junior, was critically ill. It was Jenkins who had to get up at night and administer to the baby's needs.

'The travelling and the domestic situation did not help,' Kirby was to say. 'I was criticised by the directors for not buying value for money but it was a case of a little bit for now and more later. As it happened, it all came later.'

Jenkins even struggled to score in training stints of five-a-side. 'He thought he was unlucky but he needed a more positive attitude. He got it,' said Kirby.

Mike Keen, who believed in what is dubbed 'the passing game', took over as player-manager and did not rate the beanpole striker. 'The board did not fancy Ross and they were only too keen for me to do my best and transfer him.'

Jenkins was unable to take advantage of a fresh start under the new management because he contracted a stomach illness in the last week of his holiday in Javea. He reported back for pre-season training. 'The worst of it was they did not seem to think I had a problem but, eventually after a few weeks, they sent me to Harley Street and a complication with the muscle casing was diagnosed.'

He did not enjoy a regular run in the team until February but his return of just four goals in 26 outings, along with his indifferent displays, did nothing to shift deep-rooted opinion.

Jenkins reflects on those days and admits: 'I found myself at Watford. How did that happen? I was inexperienced, leading the line and the club had paid a record fee. My anticipation and timing of movement were good: they were my main assets at the time. But it was hard to fit in.

'Under Kirby, the pattern of play was not really emphasised. We did not gel enough. Later – with John Barnes, for instance – you knew where the ball was likely to come. We worked on that but with John Farley you did not know when the cross was coming. Then Stewart Scullion joined in Mike Keen's time and, in his case, the cross might never come or, if it did, it would be beyond us all in the box.'

Jenkins' contentions with regard to service are valid. Bobby Downes and, to a degree, Brian Pollard would provide decent service and this was later enhanced when Nigel Callaghan and Barnes were on the flanks. Jenkins profited from them. As against that, in Keen's first season, Billy Jennings did not find that Farley/Scullion service a handicap as he scored 29 goals in 47 appearances. One wonders how well he would have fared had the service been better.

Keen, concerned about Jennings' lack of work-rate, dropped him and brought in the all-action Jenkins but the lack of goals forced the manager to turn to Jennings again.

At the time, Ross was being paid between £40 and £45 a week, lived in a club house and had used his £1,000 signing-on fee to place a deposit on an apartment in Javea.

'That decision has provided us with the mainstay of our lives ever since. We spent every close season there and now we are permanent residents,' says Jenkins, who found the policies at Watford as baffling as his own struggles. 'I remember, for instance, Keen bought Alan Mayes and said he was one for the future. I never bought into that idea. For me the future was Saturday so, despite the low times with the team and my own personal game, I wanted to be in the team on Saturday because Saturday was the start of the future.'

The door opened the following season when Watford sold Jennings for a club-record fee but, without Billy's goals, they slithered down the table. They compounded this by selling Pat Morrissey, a steady journeyman striker who always put in a shift, scoring 29 in 117 appearances.

'It was lean times as far as I was concerned. It was a bit of a cliquey dressing room in those days and I was not really accepted as part of the club. When Pat Morrissey left, well, that was it,' says Jenkins. 'When Deeney played well at Watford, he reminded me of Pat.'

The tall striker had an improved return of 11 goals in 34 appearances but it was not enough to arrest the decline. Watford brought in Mayes (two goals in 19) and Brian Greenhalgh (one goal in 12) but finished relegated to Division Four.

Greenhalgh had been something of a legend at Cambridge United but his tendency to freeze when he reached the penalty area earned him the nickname Snowman. He says of Jenkins: 'I remember Ross always gave 100 per cent. That fact stood out. I was going through a lean time myself but I remember being surprised he was not a better header of the ball. That came later.'

As a result the club took the unusual course of sacking coach Duggie Woodfield. It was not that he was responsible for the slump but, having been signed from Wolves by Kirby and his career effectively ended within half of his debut game at Watford, they were lumbered with Woodfield on a good contract. So Watford appointed him coach in a money-saving move and, when his contract expired, they did not renew it.

'I never knew what his philosophy was on the game because I had little do with him. It seemed an unusual move at the time, to sack a coach,' says Jenkins.

Watford's intended cost-cutting clear-out was to be completed by selling Jenkins, who had been written off. At the time, no one at Watford would have suspected he would make just shy of 400 appearances, scoring 142 goals at a ratio 2.8 games a goal, and spearhead the club to the top flight and Europe. He had been a waste of time and money, in their opinion, so when Huddersfield came in with a £12,000 bid Watford had no hesitation in accepting it, despite taking a £23,000 loss on the striker. And with that, Ross and Eve headed off for Yorkshire to talk terms.

Timber

Some might see irony in the fact the fulcrum of Graham Taylor's forward-first and high-pressing style, Ross Jenkins, should have been discovered by Arthur Rowe, celebrated author of Tottenham Hotspur's famed 'push and run', wall-pass revolution. The by then white-haired Crystal Palace scout, who had revolutionised football with his style, spotted Jenkins playing for a Brentford-based youth team. Attached to Brentford, Jenkins could not join Palace at the time but, when the Bees scrapped their training nights, Jim Jenkins, Ross's father, phoned Rowe and the youngster promptly joined Palace.

'It only involved a couple of train changes from where we lived. Sometimes my dad would take me, but Palace paid for my transport costs,' Ross remembers.

The future striker was never a football fan as such. He did not watch or attend matches and cannot recall viewing games on television. Yet almost as soon as he could walk, he had a ball at his feet and played football 'all the time, and all but living on Sheen Common'. To this day he can recall some of the goals he scored and that he was 'good' when he played in all age-group teams at his primary Brook Boys' School. To balance the boastful memory, he stresses: 'Mind you, it was a pretty small school.'

He remembers a sweet strike when he was ten years old – the ball curving into the top corner to win the district championship. 'The football pitch is still there, surrounded by trees. I see it every time I go back to England and visit my dad's resting place in the cemetery. I stand where he stood watching me hit that winner back in the days when you are young and innocent and a game seems so important, it fills your life.'

Jenkins cannot recall how, but he was recruited to Arsenal at a 'pretty young age.' 'There was no individual training. It was pretty tiring making that long trek to Arsenal and I was relieved when it ended. Somehow, I was taken on by my dad's local team, Brentford, and it was there that Arthur Rowe spotted me.'

He finished school and was signed on as an apprentice, experiencing the usual tenderfoot regimen of training in the morning and then cleaning boots, dressing rooms, kits and the ground in the afternoon. 'There were about 20 of us and we played Combination football on the Saturday morning and then cleaned up after the first team in the afternoon. I worked under Tom Walley's brother Ernie. They were very much alike. I got on well with Ernie and really liked him. We clicked from the start. We did regular weight-sessions and I believe that helped me.'

When, years later, Taylor came to Watford, Jenkins contends he was already familiar with the tactics he introduced because Ernie Walley believed in many of the same tenets. 'I believe I read the game well: seeing the moves and anticipating. There were some very good players in our reserves at Palace and they went on to make the first team as regulars.'

Jenkins' big break came in the 1971-72 campaign when Gerry Queen was injured in training and the young striker was pitched in against Manchester United, who boasted the legendary trinity: Best, Law and Charlton. Although they lost 3-1, Jenkins acquitted himself sufficiently well to enjoy a few more outings and he scored one of his 'best five goals' – a scorcher against Everton – but cut his knee open during the game.

'The Palace team was not overly attacking. I remember, somewhat harshly, a journalist claimed Palace fielded their usual 10-1 formation. I got into the side the following season but then I found myself back in the reserves after speaking out at a team meeting. I asked what other people were doing when we conceded a goal, which presumably did not go down well. I was the youngster and should keep quiet, was the attitude.'

While in the reserves, Jenkins scored four goals in one match. He did not know Watford manager Kirby was watching but the following week he was told Palace had received and accepted an offer.

'We had a glut of centre-forwards,' the Palace manager Bert Head explained. 'We were financially embarrassed. Ross had an old head for his age but lacked a little speed for the top flight.'

George Petchey was a coach at Palace and admitted Jenkins tended to go out of games when 'he was bumped a bit' but thought the player unlucky to leave Palace. That view was echoed to a degree by ex-Palace player Terry Long, who remembered Jenkins as always being keen to learn: 'The ball used to get stuck under his feet but when he filled out and got stronger, he was going places.'

Arthur Rowe was similarly disappointed but admitted: 'He was a bit stringy and a bit leggy but it was a six-to-four chance he would come on once he timbered up.'

That 'timbering up' was a significant factor, says Jenkins: 'I needed more strength. That was always the case. I needed more upper-body strength. I worked at it but I did not have a body that retained development. I would firm up what I had. I didn't put weight on. I just burned it off. Through the course of my career of course I strengthened up, but although weight-training did help, it was not the complete answer.'

He was naturally slim and remains so. Graham Taylor would explain it all in simpler terms, referring to the levers of his body maturing and Jenkins becoming more in control of his own movements.

One thing seems certain, though: the rumours persisted that Watford had chronically overpaid for Jenkins but, while Palace might have gained a good fee, there were a few at Selhurst Park who thought the striker might have a future.

That future seemed somewhat vague as the Jenkins family left Watford after 30 months to sound out what Huddersfield had to offer in the May of 1975. Terms were agreed, Eve was enthusiastic for the move and there was a feeling the striker needed to leave behind the rancid atmosphere in the Watford dressing room.

'It was obvious Keen thought Greenhalgh and Mayes would be the top strike pairing. We agreed terms and looked at houses in Huddersfield and I knew I would have to ring my decision through to the Huddersfield management in the morning. Everyone was in favour of the move. I stayed up all night mulling it over and then phoned in the morning and said "no".'

Jenkins believed he left Palace too quickly and decided he would not run again. He bought himself a new suit and returned to the club and said: 'I'm ready.' It was a pivotal decision, as Alan Mayes observed: 'Had he gone to Huddersfield he may not have ended up as First Division player. He worked at his game. He was not always the most skilful player – far from it on occasions – but he developed that skill and ended up in the top flight, looking a First Division player.'

Mike Keen was not too disappointed at Jenkins' decision: 'Everyone seemed to regard him as a bad signing, a joke. But I wasn't keen to lose him as he was a useful man to have in the squad.'

Jenkins remembers that Keen did not seem disappointed: 'Everything seemed to change from that day on. For the first time, I felt accepted. They even gave me a pay rise without my asking. People started treating me different and were far more supportive. It made all the difference or so it seemed.'

His 'intuitive decision' proved a shrewd one. A year after that trip to Huddersfield, he picked up the *Watford Observer* Player of the Season Award.

John Collins became the new coach at Vicarage Road and recalls that the striker was the best defender at set-pieces: 'Ross was everyone's fall guy in those days. If he made a mistake it was exaggerated. But he worked hard at his game under Mike and myself. I think it needed Graham Taylor to really make him believe in himself.

'I often felt if he showed the same commitment in the opposition box as he did defending set-pieces, he would make an impact. In a lap race round that ground in training, Ross would come in first.'

Jenkins forced himself into the Fourth Division line-up at Vicarage Road. The Hornets did not make an impact but performed steadily, finishing eighth in the table and Jenkins, after failing to score in the first eight, began to find the net regularly, finishing the campaign with 19 goals from 44 outings.

'Next season I will score 30,' he promised when being presented with the award, after gaining a narrow victory over second-placed Alan Garner.

It was a popular choice, however, because although fans had doubted, questioned and criticised him, they willed him to do well because of his all-action commitment. His easy-going, engaging personality had won many friends among the away-fan contingent, who found him approachable. In effect he had a dormant fan base just waiting to embrace him and his exploits.

The signing of Arthur Horsfield played a part in Jenkins' rebirth. A seasoned striker who did not have the legs that once enabled him to puncture defences regularly, he had the experience to lead the line. Later in the season, the striker moved back to the heart of defence, where he had been playing when Watford signed him from Charlton, and the emerging Keith Mercer moved from super-sub to become Jenkins' more regular partner.

Jenkins reveals: 'I found Alan Mayes very hard to read as a partner. He baffled me and he baffled a lot of others as well. He had a good partnership when he was at Swindon and I meant to go and watch them to see how it worked. I could never read him as to what he was going to do next. My best partner was Pat Morrissey and then I teamed up well for a bit with Arthur, who was an education to watch, but the partnership with Keith Mercer was even better. He went in at all angles, risking his life on occasions. We made a forceful partnership but the one with Luther was something else altogether.

'We didn't work much on pattern of play and team formation with Mike and John. At Palace, Ernie Walley always worked on that. Also, at Watford, they cut corners. The training kit was tattered: everything was done on the cheap.

'We also had a few players who did not pass to certain players. Mind you, we had some good players with Roger Joslyn, Mayesy, Andy Rankin, Keith Pritchett, Alan Garner and Bobby Downes, plus Keith Mercer was coming through. But we did not have the real structure. You need that and luck, and structure makes the luck pay off. All those players were to have success when the structure was put in place.

'Arthur played well for us but every day he had a two-and-a-half-hour journey back to Kent. That tires you out. In fact the 44-game season took its toll on me. That is an exceptional amount of games for a big fella like me. That is where going to Javea for six weeks every summer enabled me to recharge my batteries. Graham Taylor appreciated that and, after he arrived, he would encourage me to go to Spain as soon as the season ended. Not that I needed any encouragement.'

Much of Jenkins' game was beginning to come together but successive coaches, from Kirby to Taylor, wanted him to be more physical. It is somewhat ironic that people reflect on the Taylor era and fancy they recall he had a big, bustling striker who barged his way through defences and hammered defenders. But it was all an illusion. Jenkins was booked once in his career – at Brentford one evening and, as it was in front of the press box, I would state it was an overly harsh decision. Jenkins clearly agreed for he had the referee's report framed and hung in his toilet at home.

'I was tall and slim. I was not physically capable of knocking defenders flat in order to score a goal. I was not that type of player, although they kept trying to nudge me in that direction.'

He was dubbed 'the beanpole striker' and cartoonist Terry Challis in the *Watford Observer* would always depict him with the sobriquet 'Bones', wearing a shirt that was far too short with his navel invariably exposed.

He returned for the 1976-77 campaign, feeling confident, and four goals in four games justified that positivity.

'It is part of a footballer's life. One moment things are going well and things are coming together and the next moment, my career was almost finished,' he recalls.

The threat to his career was very real for, after scoring a hat-trick against Hartlepool, he returned home nursing a bruised calf. The calf started to swell and he went quickly to the Peace Memorial Hospital. The calf continued to swell and a decision was taken to cut it open.

'Effectively all the inside flopped out when the pressure was relieved by a long incision. They told me that had they not taken that action, I could have lost my leg,' reveals the striker who was out from August to October. 'They left the wound open for five days to make sure the swelling was gone and then put everything back in. Even then they had difficulty getting it all back in. It was amazing I only missed nine games with that sort of injury.'

Fourteen goals in 39 appearances was a disappointing return for Jenkins, who took some time to gain real confidence in his repaired limb. Nevertheless the partnership with Mercer proved very successful with Keith netting 25 in 52 outings to lift the Player of the Season award.

Mercer had been impressed when Jenkins congratulated him on his debut as a schoolboy against Tranmere back in 1973. 'It was unusual for a rival striker to do something like that and be so pleasant and considerate. But that is Ross. We worked well together and he really helped me win the award. I was delighted when he turned his career into a fairy tale. It couldn't have happened to a nicer bloke.'

Yet, despite that partnership, towards the end of the season Keen began to field Mercer and Mayes together with Jenkins as substitute. The big striker promptly asked for a transfer, which was granted, but soon after that Keen was axed and Jenkins withdrew his request.

In the background of these successive failures there was a little stardust. Elton John had joined the Hornets' board in 1974 and had taken over as chairman in the early summer of 1976.

'That was incredible: a world star walking into the dressing room after matches. Elton was the primary light in those days. He put the club in the papers. It was so off the wall. You know what the club was like back then: it was a really run-down Division Four outfit but Elton was our chairman. Amazing,' Jenkins reflects. 'He was the man who brought Taylor to Watford. Graham did not choose Watford: Elton lured him here and made the personal connection, convincing Graham. Elton got him and paid the £20,000 buy-out clause. That was the start of it all and the start was Elton.'

Giraffe

As did all the players in successive interviews, Jenkins met the new manager from a position of discomfort. In turn they sat awkwardly on a low seat while Graham Taylor perched above them and spelled things out very plainly.

'He told each of us that we would get a chance to prove ourselves as useful to the cause. He explained: "I am the new manager and you are going to do what I tell you to do. So you will get the chance to prove you can do the job I want you to do,"' Jenkins smiles at the memory. 'He was extremely well focused on what he believed in. He had some success with Lincoln but I had not picked up on his style. Together with Graham, Elton became more dominant, more visible and responsible and progressive. The new manager changed concepts everywhere.

'Graham had a definite plan for the way he was going to cope with Division Four and how he was going to make it work. He was extremely confident but that was it. You got off your low seat and left in no doubt that you either toed his line or you would be out.'

There followed a 'massive change' in pre-season training. Fitness and everything on the training side was geared to the requirements of a successful team. 'Physical fitness was very much the accent with an additional concentration on body and stomach, which was fine by me.' Then came the pattern of play: the formation of play and working on players' strengths.

'That was very important. He aimed to improve what we were good at and, where we had weaknesses in our game, he aimed to improve them or make them not so significant by adjusting play accordingly,' said Jenkins, who was later urged by Graham to improve his left-foot work. 'That's why I produced that left-foot shovel kick at Sheffield Wednesday in the Third Division run-in,' he adds with a rueful smile.

Taylor varied the venues for training but when you arrived at a new one, you knew it was going to be a long session: 'Could he talk! Gordon Bennett, he could talk. For two hours you would run around and learn and practise what he had told you. We would have a half-hour break and we would come back. It was almost obsessive. You weren't going to get off that training pitch until Graham was satisfied that we had taken in the exercises and lessons. Only then could you pack up and go home.'

The contrast was immediate: 'Keeney was never quite sure what team he was going to pick and how they were going to play. He did not work on gelling the team. He was a consummate player himself – a good man and I had a lot of time for him – but there was not that drive, motivation and sense of direction. Mike was a little short on that, as was George Kirby.

'Graham created this environment that if you performed you would play. We all had to be part of the team and the pattern. Individual players were like those in a band; you could play a drum solo but Graham did not want too much. He was focused on playing in a certain way. Within that you could be individual as long as it did not compromise the overall team ethic.

'In a way, we each became individuals within that system because we became good at it. In time it was like putting on your favourite CD. You enjoy it, you know what comes next but you know where you have to be and what you have to do. There was room for skill, ability and individuality but the most important thing was the team. He challenged you, such as training out in the rain. He never over-praised you but you knew you were doing it if he picked you.'

Taylor improved every player, working on Jenkins with Bolton sending 40-yard passes to his chest or feet so developing and vastly improving what had been, up until then, haphazard control. He also solved the long-running problem of the tall player not being as impressive in the air as he ought to be. Taylor decided, as Jenkins was not good at a standing jump, to encourage him to arrive in the danger zone later, so gaining a run to aid his jump. The effect was almost immediate.

'He worked on so many things, repeatedly. They were like drills we worked on so eventually if someone stopped the game, you could point blindfolded to where each of your colleagues was. Everything in attack was with a view to getting a cross, a shot or a header.'

Taylor was soon to observe Jenkins was an intelligent footballer as he deployed the striker as a magnet for defenders, enabling others to attack the ball without receiving such fierce challenges.

'You would go in on a Monday morning after a game and you knew you would be working on certain things. It was very much a team culture, a team responsibility, and he created a very strong team ethic. He was the pied piper and we followed him.'

Taylor made it very clear that he knew where he was going: to the top. The question was as to who was going with him. The four who finally made it from Division Four to Division One – the Rocket Men – each hoped they would make the complete journey but at that time they did not know if that meant the Third or Second Divisions.

'I don't think we thought in terms of playing in the top flight. We just set promotion as the target and then refocused when it was achieved. In a sense Graham announced there was a train going to the top and questioned did we want to join him on the journey? The majority got on that train and headed for Division Three and beyond.

'I was very happy in that environment. I think I surprised Graham with what I could actually achieve. I think he considered I was not the answer to what he wanted up front. He did say he had inherited a team "with a bloody giraffe as striker".'

Taylor had written a breakdown on the Watford team prior to taking them on when he was manager at Lincoln. In his 1975 brief he told his Lincoln players Jenkins was not overly aggressive, seemed popular with certain sections of supporters, and never gave up despite being deployed to fight a lone battle up front. He also pinpointed the fact that Jenkins would always go to his right and favoured his right foot but it was important not to try and out-head him when the odds were stacked against you because that would lead to free-kicks. Taylor hated conceding free-kicks.

At the end of the first season, Taylor would be far more positive in assessing Jenkins, including the observation that the player was far more intelligent than his slow somewhat laconic delivery would sometimes suggest. In fact, Jenkins has always thought before opening his mouth and this – combined with a fixed, focused stare – sometimes unnerved Taylor throughout their relationship because the manager could never quite fathom what the big man was thinking.

Taylor was not the first, for Mike Keen would try to avoid Jenkins' stare. When coach Collins had called all the first-team squad down the other end of the pitch one morning, Keen had positioned himself behind Ross and said quietly: 'You stay this end, Ross.' A face-to-face confrontation and that stare had been avoided.

When Taylor told Jenkins he was dropped, the striker would fix him with a stare and announce: 'That's a mistake.'

At times, Taylor would bounce a few thoughts on Jenkins off me, as if I had the key to the striker's psyche because we were friends. Reflecting on the Division Four season, Taylor said: 'He is a very willing runner with an appetite for work. He is always willing to make runs even if the ball does not always come to him. He knows his finishing leaves a little to be desired. At 6ft 4ins you have to be a problem. You get given 12 goals a season with that height. I would like to see him throw his size about more and not get knocked off the ball so easily.'

Jenkins was not pleased with the concept of 'being given 12 goals a season' because of his size. 'I have never been given goals. You have to work for them but my finishing did improve. I scored a lot of scrappy goals earlier on in my career but subsequently I began to strike the ball cleanly.' Those levers were beginning to work in harmony.

Back in the early Taylor days, Jenkins found himself repeatedly fouled by Sam Ellis during practice games.

'He really went in hard,' the striker recalls and he may have been tempted to think this was an effort to rile him, toughen him up or to get him to throw his body about. Such theories appeared to be scotched when, after a particularly bad tackle by the skipper, Taylor immediately ordered Ellis to return to the ground.

'We were at Shendish. We had changed at the ground, been driven up so Sam had to set off in his football boots and shorts. We were in the team bus and we passed him striding through Langleybury in his boots: the steam still coming out of his ears.'

The publicity surrounding Elton and Taylor resulted in the Division Four players appreciating that they too were, to a degree, fashionable with the supporters. The community drive, led by Taylor, also involved the players. While it is always easier when you are winning, the players enjoyed meeting the fans and taking part in community events.

'I always got on well with the travelling supporters. I always talked to them even when I was the scapegoat and they did not think I would ever be the answer to their prayers. I believed in that community aspect and work in the community. I enjoyed going to the functions and meeting people. It knitted the community together.

'The Fourth Division was so hard, regarding the physical elements you were up against. I might be wrong but it was my impression that the Fourth campaign did not include overly attractive football. We won it well but all the time we were knitting a team together and learning what Graham wanted. Even with the championship won, there were still elements that were not right.'

Taylor would often explode with rage over poor performances. 'I never received a rollicking. I remember Boothy had one once. We had the tea going round the dressing room after GT swiped at it, so you learned never to wear your best suit. I like a cup of tea, but in a mug.

'To be fair, on most occasions he would try to tweak what we had done. We didn't have many personal conversations: he just kept picking me. I was totally behind him in that I believed it was a good way to play the game. When we won the Division Four title, he did not cuddle or congratulate you. I think the respect for him grew among the players and respect for each other as well. He generated the desire to do well and follow his hard-work ethic . . . what was wrong with that?'

Looking back at the end of the 1977-78 campaign, Jenkins was quoted as saying that the club always had good players at Vicarage Road but 'now they are better managed'. He said the players began to believe this was their year after the 3-0 victory at Brentford in early October: 'We never thought we would lose that lead at the top.'

Jenkins played 45 games, scored 17 goals, with Luther Blissett scoring six goals in 36 outings, 16 of those appearances from the bench. Alan Mayes hit 16 in 49 and Keith Mercer netted 13 in 26. However, Graham Taylor, looking ahead to Division Three, was not that impressed with the tallies. He felt the need to improve his strike force – a decision that proved to be one of his few misjudgements during a ten-year spell as manager, although not the last involving Jenkins.

Mercer's career was severely handicapped by a horrific knee injury and Mayes left for promotion rivals Swindon some eight months later. It transpired, while Watford scouts were out looking for potential strikers, Watford's two-pronged strike force of Jenkins and Blissett proved eminently up to the challenge, scoring more goals as a partnership than any duo since the famed Cliff Holton and Dennis Uphill in 1959-60.

For the record, Uphill scored 36 in 52 and Holton a prodigious 48 in 53. Jenkins hit 37 in 58 and Blissett 28 in 49 during the course of the 1978-79 season. In the annals of Watford's history, apart from Holton and Uphill, only Leftie McPherson (35), Holton again (34), Fred Pagnam (32), George James/ Maurice Cook (31) and Dai Ward (30) had reached the 30-mark in a campaign. So Jenkins had racked up the second-highest total of goals in a season, sandwiched by the prolific Holton and Uphill. Fittingly, when Jenkins won Player of the Season in May 1979, Holton was there to present the award.

'When I first saw Luther, I knew he was exceptionally fit,' says Jenkins. 'The ball could bounce off him but he knocked it forward. Because of his pace, he would be frightening, getting beyond and behind people and hurting teams.

'He was young and a talent in the making. He had potential but we did not know how much. In that Third Division campaign, he showed us what he could do. He made the most of his opportunity. Keith Mercer worked so hard, was sometimes reckless but he paid heavily for his bravery and that opened the door for Luther.'

Jenkins looks back on that season and regards it as the icing on the cake. 'I think that was the result of all the hard work we had undertaken in Division Four. We were a unit, well-drilled and we knew what to do. So when we started in Division Three, we were confident and soon led the division. To us it seemed business as usual.

'I think Luther's emergence was a surprise to everybody, but twin strikers working together so very well was a bonus. We didn't have to work at our understanding too much. That came naturally; it was intuitive but we had to work on the tactics on the training pitch – the cross-overs and identifying which were our respective zones. He was young and I was experienced, dragging the defence about. We complemented each other in that he made me look good because I could flick the ball on and I knew where he was without looking. In fact, we made each other look good.

'I always liked Luther a lot as a person so we gelled very easily as players. Our team shape and form were already in place. I could control the ball and lay it off or back and Luther grew in confidence. He might not get it under full control but it was the pace that totally unsettled the defences. However, he also took time getting the timing right and not being caught offside.

'We worked at the cross-overs, running towards the halfway line in an arc so I would come in from the Main Stand side and head out towards Shrodells with my marker chasing. Luther would do the opposite. It was right up my street, leading players away from their comfort zone. You know what you are doing and you do it with confidence, which is a big thing. Confidence makes such a difference and people probably thought I was a different player. In some respects I was. My heading had improved and become more forceful, whereas previously I had tended to let the ball hit my head and loop forward. That season was my watershed. My game came together a lot during that season and I became confident about every aspect of my game.'

Jenkins was firmly on Taylor's train by then. 'A few jumped off and a few jumped on but the train was still moving forward. From what we had been, what I had gone through along with some of the other players, to find yourself a part of something that was gathering momentum all the way, made it a special time. The Third Division was a turning point. We opened people's eyes.'

One of the big eye-openers was third-tier Watford knocking Manchester United out of the League Cup at Old Trafford. Taylor was sarcastic to his players at half-time, suggesting if they hung on to a 1-0 defeat they would not have done badly for, after all, they were not expected to win. They could go home 1-0 losers or: 'You can go out there and represent me properly and get some crosses in.'

Jenkins remembers the half-time pep talk but wonders if it was that or two headers from the then-unlikely source of Blissett that turned the tables. Either way, they were both scored from crosses. 'They were two lovely headers. We stayed and watched the game on telly before coming home.'

Jenkins also questioned the wisdom of Taylor's decision to change a few things. Ray Train and Steve Sims were brought in and Watford began to falter a little, for they had a League Cup team that bowed out in the semi-finals over two legs to Nottingham Forest, and the League side that included the two new recruits.

'I think he was looking to replace Roger, but Jos played really well and expressed himself. Also, when you played in those days and were out for a few weeks, you didn't see another £1 million going in the bank while you were receiving treatment, as they do now. It was very important to get back and, if you could avoid it, not let a minor injury rule you out.

'You think back to that team that took on First Division sides in the Cup and led the division. We were so close. That squad, in my opinion, could have gone on but I wasn't in Taylor's position sitting on the side and watching it. But he took an ingredient out, put another in and it wasn't the same taste. You try and improve something that does not need improving. It is arguable but he seemed happy to pay for the players who would stand him in good stead in Division Two. I mean, someone like Ray Train added to the mix but he also lacked some things his predecessor had. You improved but at the same time lost something.'

Watford's League Cup run was a bonus but Forest, after a 3-1 first-leg victory, closed the game down in the second leg 0-0 at Vicarage Road. 'You had to admire what Cloughie did. He signed good pros who could do the right things at the right time. They were a first-class professional team. But it was an enjoyable run.'

The Third Division campaign included plenty of good, creative and attacking football. 'Even the away trips were better than they were in the Fourth Division, where you travelled for hours, came to a dingy dressing room through a door at the back of the stand and tested whether the nail in the wall would take your jacket.'

By then the 6ft 3in Jenkins had grown to 6ft 4ins. 'I don't know when that happened. I think it was probably down to Graham's stretching exercises.'

Not surprisingly, with 37 goals in his locker, Jenkins won Player of the Season in 1979. 'He's up there with the Holtons and the Barnetts. He is one of the club's all-time greats,' said Elton John, adding: 'And I never thought I'd be saying that.' Later the chairman would admit that when the club gained promotion to the top flight, Jenkins was one of the first people he thought about. 'It was down to sheer determination, intense hard work and his playing ability has improved as well.'

Around that time I bumped into George Kirby who asked: 'Is he up with the Holtons and Barnetts now?' Touché.

Although Watford staggered towards the end of that campaign, they won at Sheffield Wednesday, with Jenkins scoring with a mis-hit left-foot shot, and then romped 4-0 to victory over Hull at Vicarage Road to clinch second spot and promotion.

Says Jenkins: 'I would like to think those four goalscorers against Hull summed up that season: Luther and I, Bolts and Roger Joslyn. What a great performance by Roger at Hillsborough. He was brilliant. It was a great season. Luther and I were scoring all the goals and getting the attention, and the midfield players were doing all the work and few people noticed. It was an enjoyable season despite the wobble and it was one, like the Fourth Division campaign, that was full of hard work. The intensity of that work was eased by the likes of Dennis Booth and later Steve Harrison as well. They brought plenty of laughter and relaxed the tension. They both had excellent talents for mimicry and at times they lightened the mood. Graham would sometimes come into the dressing room during matches with the vein in his neck pulsing, his chest out and lacking only flames coming out of his mouth. After such occasions, the two jokers would break the ice.

'Then there was a time he did not come in and Boothy and Harrison mimicked him, telling us what we needed to do. They were spot on. Just before we went out for the second half, Graham comes in and says: "Well, those two have told you what to do, so go out and do it."'

Taylor, reviewing the campaign, admitted: 'The big man has been a revelation. I love front players and that is coming from a former full-back. Ross's goals, displays and everything were beyond our expectation. He scored a lot of goals with his head and he is still improving in the air. His work in and around the vital areas has been great and his control, particularly with his chest, has been brilliant. He was essentially a substitute when I came here, but I just couldn't see how a man at 6ft 4ins couldn't be a problem to defences.' Their relationship was never going to be totally smooth, for Taylor was never quite sure what the big man with the penetrating stare was really thinking.

Majestic

And so to the Second Division or as Jenkins put it: 'Another hill to climb and they kept getting steeper.'

The statistics show that Watford finished 18th out of 22 in that first season in the second tier and Jenkins had only five goals to his name while Blissett had 11.

'I had an ankle break and was out from October to the end of January. We lost Bobby Downes and Brian Pollard so we did not have the width, which we needed. Luther ended up playing out wide. We also lost Roger Joslyn, Keith Mercer and Alan Garner. The oil in the works had thickened up and the engine was grinding a bit. We had to raise our performances in Division Two because, if you don't, the deficiencies are highlighted more.'

Jenkins has doubts over the need for that clear-out which, in retrospect, Taylor shared: 'I think Graham felt we had to play tidier football and we lost important elements of the pivotal game plan. Parts of it remained but the fact is he moved players on for money, who were still of use. I think, when you bring players in, you add to your problems. The players brought into Division Two were more set in their ways of playing and weren't able to adjust to the system we were employing. It was the same for Malcolm Poskett who we brought in. Graham was in new territory managerially and was being tested, as were all the players. You say Graham admitted later he broke the side up too soon and I would agree with that.'

They struggled in Division Two for 18 months before Graham began to find the key to progress. But it was not always a struggle, for there were also two memorable League Cup successes: 7-1 versus the Football League leaders Southampton and 4-1 against the European Champions, Nottingham Forest.

Jenkins admits that he also had that old feeling of the team clicking into gear in the famous League Cup victory over Southampton on a tumultuous evening: 'Southampton at home: all the ingredients came out that night, doing their bit to make the meal really good. Everyone played to the summit and it was hard to live with if we were really on song in those days.

'We really didn't perform at all down there at The Dell. I was left on the bench, which I had told him was a mistake, as usual. They were comfortable winners of the first leg and there was the feeling they only had to get off the bus, play a bit and they would be through to the next round. But we were ready for them. We didn't have many defeats like that 4-0 pasting. The atmosphere for the second leg was top-notch and the intensity of the game was right there from the beginning. We were looking to score two in each half and we started from the kick-off to a pre-set plan. Before the end Southampton's star, Charlie George, wanted to get off.'

Jenkins, voted Man of the Match, scored the goal that took the match into extra-time. 'I was coming in at the far post and the ball was bouncing. My aim in that shot was to keep it low and not sky it, and it went past the keeper inside the post. That was another of my top-five goals,' he admits. 'In a sense, even back then, you knew there was no reason why that team could not go out and do that in the top flight.'

Again Jenkins became the hero, with a supreme supporting cast, when he scored a hat-trick against Nottingham Forest in a 4-1 win in a subsequent round: 'Against Forest, I think it was more the defence that played so well. We had a lot of possession during that game. It must be a credit to the defence. I recall the goals. I had a shot and was fortunate but two of them were very good goals. It was such a vibrant night. The fans seemed to be that much more exuberant.'

It was a week before his 29th birthday and, after taking the match ball home, Ross – with the adrenalin still running – celebrated by staying up until 2 a.m. . . . wallpapering because he could not sleep. It had been 23 months since his last hat-trick.

'I scored one with my left foot,' he stressed to the press after the game, knowing Taylor felt he was too right-footed. It was a powerful shot to a rebound, and another goal was scored when the ball came to him in space: 'It all went quiet and I just concentrated on putting it in.' A deft, Blissett-headed pass set him up for the other goal in his hat-trick.

Despite those cup heroics, Watford had not started the second season in Division Two well, but by November Taylor had brought in Les Taylor, Gerry Armstrong and Pat Rice.

'Pat was professional and did a solid, efficient, reliable job. He was not that sociable but was here to do a job and did it. He knew how to cover and be in the right place at the right time, but scampering up the touchline was not his forte. Les Taylor was very accomplished and proved to be a valuable player for the club. He always gave 100 per cent to hold us together and continued to do so. His vision with passing was far greater than he was given credit for.

'Then there was Gerry Armstrong who was brought in to replace me or kick me up the backside. So Graham couldn't lose. He was an exceptionally nice man. He wore his heart on his sleeve. Gerry was best with the ball at his feet and he would leave a groove in the pitch when he went through defences. In the end he was a great and ideal substitute who could help to change games.'

Jenkins felt the manager had lost his way since reaching Division Two, because of the lack of effective width, which had been so essential in the previous two divisions. He also believed the manager was writing him off too soon.

'I didn't think it was time for me to get off the train. I had a lot more about my game than people realised. I think there was always a doubt with me and indeed everybody, whether I would do it in the higher division. That is part of living: can you measure up, meet the challenge, be successful? Every year perhaps a tenth of your career slips by and the questions grow, I suppose.'

Watford did not have much in the way of width that season, although disappointing winger, Wilf Rostron, was switched to become a very impressive full-back.

'He was like a little terrier biting at everyone as he ran around. He was physically a very strong player who worked at that position. I can never remember Graham, in all those years, working with the defensive aspect of the team. It was always attack,' Jenkins recalls.

He felt the new players had grown into the team: 'Simsy was like Keith Mercer – he had a glass knee, which prevented him from having an even greater impact. They had knee-ligament injuries, which handicapped them, but Simsy had a way of jumping and heading the ball away without the opponent, jumping with him, being able to make any impression.

'Steve Sherwood they thought was too gentle a giant but he matured as a player, made great shot-stops and could claim crosses. He got a memorable football career and was a very nice man and a very good trainer.'

Nevertheless, Jenkins felt he had been written off, and argued that if the team had width and provided a service, he would deliver the goods. He was less than pleased when placed on the transfer list for £100,000, signalling the end of the line. He had scored nine in 30 appearances that season but Taylor wanted to make room for Armstrong.

Said Taylor: 'Ross was not playing too well. And no one came in for him, suggesting other clubs felt he wasn't playing too well either. The biggest mistake was made by the clubs who didn't buy him. They missed a trick.'

Ian Bolton felt that perhaps the Gaffer had missed a trick too: a rare error by the man he admired. In fact, another consideration was that Bolton was out for four months during that period, so Jenkins lacked another source of service. As one insider put it when seeing the Bolton-less team: 'I know Ross is supposed to be 10ft tall but I didn't realise he was supposed to be 20ft wide.' That was a clear reflection of how others lacked Bolton's accuracy in hitting the pass upfield, as they tried making up for the centre-half's absence.

Today Jenkins cannot recall having been on the list with a six-figure price tag but that is what happened. Personally, I believe the former striker had a point. Watford had eased away from the old shape of two men wide and two central strikers. That was confirmed eight months later when, with Barnes and Callaghan, Taylor suddenly saw his old shape back and was pleased with the way they had played because 'we had not worked on that pattern in training'.

'In the end, I engineered a move. It was funny. I was a bit down when I left Watford. I think the rumour about Graham and I not getting on was because he kept dropping me,' he joked a year later. 'We had and have a good understanding and

I respect and admire what he has done. There was no case of us having a bust-up. I made my decision based on the fact you do feel a bit put out when he excludes you from the team. I felt I could do it in Division Two, but he seemed to have other ideas.'

Taylor stressed: 'There was never any clash. I made my decision based on the circumstances at the time.'

The clash of beliefs rather than personalities between Jenkins and Taylor resulted in the striker being loaned out to Washington Diplomats, managed by ex-Hornet Ken Furphy. They discovered a loan deal was not permitted so Washington paid a fee and received it back from Watford at the end of their season, in an agreement between true gentlemen.

'I was offered good money. It was never going to be permanent and, at the end of their season, I came back having missed out on Watford's pre-season.

'It was a strange set-up in the US. The game was being sold; the crowds weren't big and you got on a plane, not a coach, and flew, landed and were taken to an Astroturf stadium. I enjoyed it, flying all around the USA and parts of Canada. When we flew home it would be a bit hairy because you would come into land between two skyscrapers.

'I scored one of my best-ever goals – rifling the ball in against New York Cosmos. It was a truly stunning goal, when everything went right: hit with such incredible power, it lifted the net. The other highlight for me was when they brought Johan Cruyff in to attract the crowds. He was slim with an unbelievable physique. He couldn't run then – the injuries had caught up with him – but even in that state you could see what he had been. He was class – crème de la crème. He scored one goal from the halfway line.'

Jenkins and Furphy got on well but in the end the striker returned to Watford: 'Ready to play my part.'

Taylor thought Jenkins returned a changed man, arguing that the player had become stale after being at Watford since 1972. 'He had a chance to see that the grass is not that greener on the other side.'

If people thought the team had moved on without him, that changed when Taylor decided to play him against Chelsea at Stamford Bridge. Was it a backward step? 'If he doesn't do it now, he never will,' said the manager before the game. Taylor subsequently admitted that he had found his pattern at Chelsea that afternoon. So by that remark, Taylor was admitting he had shelved much of that pattern after Division Three.

Jenkins recalls he came back to Watford and noted a subtle change in the manager's demeanour. 'He gave me the recognition after that. The eye contact, the nod; we could read the eyes. I thought that he had been going down the wrong road. I always thought I could do what he wanted and I did not think there was anything or anyone better than me at achieving that. He never said well done for doing something you were expected to go out and do. We didn't go in for long conversations.'

Taylor was later to say, after promotion was attained: 'Contrary to some rumours, we get on very well. He keeps on coming back and he led the line so well once again.'

At Chelsea, Jenkins had lined up with Barnes, Armstrong and Callaghan in a front line that boasted width.

'I knew what Nigel could do but when I saw Barnesy, I thought: "Hello, I have been waiting for you, pal."'

Watford fielded two effective men wide. Taylor saw it: the old shape, the old formation, with Barnes making his first start. Watford won 3-1 at Stamford Bridge, with Jenkins assisting all three goals, and when the suspended Blissett returned to the side, he had the old familiar formation back – this time with Callaghan, Blissett, Jenkins and Barnes.

'Barnesy was just tiptoeing through tulips. He had amazing and natural talent. He was in tune with the ball, even when it was bouncing. He seemed to be able to bounce with it and when he arrived, the position was waiting for him,' enthuses Jenkins.

'Cally was the little magician on the flank. When you looked at him it seemed like he had just taken his school uniform off and come to play. He could twist a full-back into the ground and hit lovely crosses. I loved Nigel and those beautiful crosses. You knew exactly where he was going to hit it. The Boss was always working on him getting the ball before the full-back could nail him.

'Another player who established himself in midfield was Kenny Jackett. He was steady and good at changing the direction of play. A student of the game, he worked well, tackled well and he must have walked off the pitch after every game, knowing he would be picked the next week. Like Bolts, he always seemed to have something in reserve.'

Mention of Bolton prompts Jenkins to wax really lyrical because while the Jenkins–Blissett partnership gained fame, Bolton was an essential contributor to their success. 'I have never seen anyone hit cannonball passes like Bolts did: straight to your chest, head or feet from anything up to 50 yards. The trajectory was remarkable. He didn't loft the ball because that would have played into the hands of the defenders. He drilled those cannonballs, notifying me before he struck it: "Get on the end of this, Ross." I knew where it was going and was able to meet it.

'Everyone knew where it was going and would move up in support. I am glad he won Player of the Season one year because his was a key ingredient to our play. He hit a long pass, not a long ball. He also had a very quick turn of pace and could nip in front of people. He made that position his own and those passes were of a quality and a trajectory that I have never seen replicated.'

Jenkins stresses the camaraderie of that squad was excellent: 'Everyone knew it was working and where we were going. Even Gerry was happy because he could come on and do his bit. There were periods that season when we were the best we could be, and I am talking about my partnership with Luther.

'I think we frightened teams. What do you tell your centre-halves to do, especially as we were moving them around? I had the feeling that nothing was going to stop us from being effective and that drive and belief was an ingredient in all three promotions and on into the top flight.

'It was a pleasure to be there. You thought: "I can do this, we can do this and we can win." All that old Third Division confidence and swagger came back into our play. We knew the system worked.'

Fittingly, Watford's first-ever promotion to the top flight was completed one Tuesday night against Wrexham with two games to spare, and Jenkins scored both goals in the 2-0 victory: 'I was feeling really confident and I had been able to pass that on to the younger players. It was nice to score both goals in a 2-0 success. I cannot recall the goals clearly but I cherish them among my top five because of what they achieved.'

As it happened, his second goal, virtually confirming promotion, prompted a premature pitch invasion.

'I was still on the train and we were heading into what was, for the club, uncharted territory and what was, for me, back to where my League career had started. It had taken me a whole career to make that round trip.'

He had scored 15 goals in 39 appearances but it was his leadership of the line that was so impressive.

The effective width of Callaghan and Barnes, the intuitive partnership of Jenkins and Blissett, plus those arrowing passes from deep from Bolton, were only too familiar to the Watford faithful, and happily so. But something more had happened. The timbering-up of Ross Jenkins had long been accomplished. The rangy striker had put in performances and leadership of the line that had no true equal in Watford's history.

He was certainly the best line-leader I ever witnessed at Vicarage Road, and the only one to run him close was Charlie Livesey in his one brilliant season. Charlie had more natural talent and physicality, but Jenkins, with his growing confidence and realisation of his long-held inner belief, developed a quality that I for one never expected to attribute to him: he was, on occasions, majestic.

One did not imagine ever seeing Jenkins out on the touchline, dummying a defender and then going past him, but we all saw it as the man once dubbed Watford's ugly duckling developed into a swan. He knew what he was doing and we were privileged to see a man forged by setbacks and ridicule, come through and display a host of skills in the mastery of the art of a line-leader. By then he had established himself among the club's elite – and deservedly so. I remember shaking my head in the press box early the following season and smiling at the sight of him sending in full-blooded drives on the Sunderland goal. His levers had 'timbered up' to perfection.

There were so many qualities overlooked in that Second Division side who finished runners-up to Luton, but among the most inspiring was Jenkins' demonstration of the art of centre-forward play without ever having to rely on physicality or bullying his opponents.

As you delighted watching him stride the Vicarage Road turf with authority, his presence and his emergence somehow typified Watford's rise from the ashes of Division Four where, a few years earlier at Darlington, he had played in the side that briefly found itself at the bottom of the Football League.

The outfit which had struggled with a dilapidated dog track and 'a giraffe of a striker' had metamorphosed into a stylish club that was as innovative off the field as it was effective on it. And leading that charge was the man who epitomised that transformation, for Jenkins had once looked as unfashionable as the club, and the fans identified with the symbolism of his and the club's elevation in unison from the depths. We had made the journey together to realise the unlikely: 'the impossible dream'.

When Jenkins left Watford, Taylor wrote in the player's testimonial brochure that he was 'one of the most underestimated front runners in the game today. Because of his height it is easy to recognise he must be a threat in the air but too many people think this is the only threat he poses. He has excellent ability to lead the line, making himself available for all his colleagues to find him.

'His control with his back to the goal has improved out of all recognition, while the timing of his runs in and behind defenders is of the highest standard. He knows how to pull away from defenders – especially in the penalty box, thereby creating space for either himself or a team-mate.

'Do not be fooled by the fact he is not the smoothest mover – at 6ft 4in he is bound to be ungainly at times. This also on occasions prevents him from snapping up the very sharp, loose chances that occur in the goal area – but this is a small price to pay for a man who can now be truly termed a bloody good centre-forward.'

Taylor went on to point out that there had been many centre-halves from Division Four to the top flight who had not been able to contain him. He also compared the partnership of Jenkins and Blissett in 1982 with that of Portugal's Torres and Eusebio from the World Cup of 1966.

It was high praise indeed as Jenkins celebrated his own testimonial season and the end of that 'train' journey to the top flight. There were many managers who had witnessed his development who relished the prospect of their centre-halves rattling him, but they – as with their predecessors – were to be disappointed.

Taylor had asked them, back in the Fourth Division, which of them were going to the top with him. Four of them had met the challenge and made it: the Rocket Men. For Jenkins there was no doubt as to who deserved the credit: 'Go to Vicarage Road now and there are two stands named after them. It was an overdue gesture. Elton and Graham fully deserved those stands being named after them. That was a remarkable achievement.'

* * *

It was hot in Norway. They were experiencing their biggest heatwave since 1909 when Watford landed for pre-season training before taking on the might of the top flight.

'It was a strange environment like an isolation camp,' Jenkins remembers. 'The training was intensive stuff with morning, afternoon and evening sessions. Graham was a hard taskmaster at team formation and pattern of play. Our location was remote. There was nowhere else to go. We were locked in there in isolation and it worked, as we once again learned to all operate together.

'We came back exceptionally fit. I never recall a time in any of those matches in those days when we were deadbeat. We never were tired, yet only last season I remember seeing on TV a Crystal Palace player run the length of the field, shoot and then collapse on the field. We did not do that. I could imagine Graham jumping up from the bench, flames coming out of his mouth if we ever did that, but he made sure it was never remotely a possibility. We were that fit.

'We worked hard in a positive sense because we were looking to score, always looking to score. If you are chasing the ball because the opposition has it, that can be tiring but if you are breaking forward, looking to score, that is uplifting.

'The training was painful at times but it was done with a view to increasing our cardiovascular potential. When I look at footballers today, a lot of teams are not as physically fit as they should be.'

Jenkins recalls Watford coming in for criticism for their so-called 'route-one philosophy': 'It was very silly to criticise things negatively. I think they really took it out on Graham because they said he was wrong and then he proved them wrong. They were criticising something that was working and entertaining. So who were they? It was like Manchester United under Fergie: attacking at every opportunity. Didn't Liverpool in their heyday have two players coming down the flanks and two blokes in the centre going for it? We played and lost at Liverpool but after the game, when we looked at the stats the next week, they had hit more long balls than we did. Strange that: it never got mentioned outside Watford.'

Watford finished that season second to Liverpool. This outrageous achievement included some memorable victories, such as the 8-0 demolition of Sunderland and a last-day defeat of the leaders. During the Sunderland game, the visiting keeper Chris Turner put in a class display to keep the score down to eight, and he made three spectacular saves from shots powerfully struck by Jenkins – a player at the top of his game.

It was Jenkins' testimonial year but unfortunately it was also to be his Watford swansong. He made 26 outings that season, played well and even scored twice in the 7-3 defeat at Nottingham Forest in the League Cup. It was poignant that his last game was against Everton – the club against whom he scored his first goal for Palace all those years previously.

'It was against Tottenham at White Hart Lane at the beginning of November. I felt something go in my stomach during the game. We won 1-0, courtesy of Les Taylor. Initially they did not think it was serious and I played in mid-week scoring those two against Forest, but then I started to miss the odd game. Stretching to score in that game made things worse.'

Jenkins was rested and then worked, but when he had to turn or twist, the pain in his stomach returned.

'It reduced my movement. To be honest, I was never happy with their diagnosis. It proved to be a hernia but they thought otherwise at the time. They thought it was irreversible wear and tear at the base of my pelvis. But it was not. Rest was never going to make it better. If they had scans in those days, I would have been operated on and been back. I felt good enough for at least a couple more years. Sadly the diagnosis was wrong.'

Jenkins was rested during the week and brought out like a Trojan horse and placed in the opposition half to frighten the opponents. He made nine more appearances in the next 13 games.

'It went on so long, Graham rearranged the team and it went on winning. There was a lot going on with my testimonial. My contract was running out and I had seen other players released so, as I was not among them, I expected the offer of a new deal. We realised when we had finished second to Liverpool, who were a special team, that we had achieved a real milestone on top of all the rest. I watched as we beat them at the end of the season. There was the feeling that we had achieved a magnificent position, but it was bittersweet in a sense.

'That morning Graham had told me that the train was going on but it was my turn: while the train moved on, I was to be left on the platform.'

* * *

Ross Jenkins was the only Watford player, in the club's history, who took in the view from the bottom of the pile – 92nd in the Football League – and the summit: top of the First Division.

Three games into the 1975-76 season, he played in the 1-0 defeat at Darlington which left the Hornets briefly carrying the wooden spoon in the Fourth Division. And although he missed out through injury 2,569 days later, in September 1982, when a 3-0 win against West Bromwich Albion sent Watford top of the League for the only weekend in 136 years of the club's existence, Jenkins came off the bench when Graham Taylor's side visited Nottingham Forest at No.1 in the charts the following week.

Division Four table, 30 August 1975

	P	W	D	L	F	A	Pts
Darlington	3	3	0	0	5	1	6
Barnsley	3	2	1	0	4	1	5
Newport County	3	2	1	0	5	2	5
Reading	3	2	1	0	6	3	5
Huddersfield Town	3	1	2	0	3	1	4
Tranmere Rovers	3	1	2	0	5	3	4
Exeter City	3	2	0	1	3	2	4
Brentford	3	1	2	0	5	4	4
Cambridge United	3	1	1	1	2	1	3
Stockport County	3	1	1	1	5	4	3
Bournemouth	3	1	1	1	3	3	3
Doncaster Rovers	3	1	1	1	5	5	3
Hartlepool United	3	0	3	0	4	4	3
Lincoln City	3	1	1	1	7	7	3
Northampton Town	3	1	1	1	5	5	3
Swansea City	3	1	1	1	3	3	3
Rochdale	3	1	1	1	2	3	3
Torquay United	3	1	0	2	5	7	2
Crewe Alexandra	3	0	2	1	4	6	2
Bradford City	3	0	2	1	1	2	2
Scunthorpe United	3	0	1	2	0	3	1
Southport	3	0	1	2	0	3	1
Workington	3	0	0	3	2	7	0
WATFORD	3	0	0	3	0	4	0

Two points for a win, teams on same points separated by goal average

Seven years, 12 days and 91 places later . . .

Division One table, 11 September 1982

	P	W	D	L	F	A	Pts
WATFORD	5	4	0	1	11	3	12
Manchester United	5	4	0	1	12	5	12
Manchester City	5	4	0	1	6	3	12
Liverpool	5	3	2	0	11	6	11
West Bromwich Albion	5	3	0	2	11	6	9
Stoke City	5	3	0	2	10	7	9
Notts County	5	2	2	1	6	6	8
West Ham United	5	2	1	2	9	4	7
Tottenham Hotspur	5	2	1	2	12	8	7
Swansea City	5	2	1	2	8	7	7
Sunderland	5	2	1	2	7	6	7
Coventry City	5	2	1	2	4	5	7
Brighton	5	2	1	2	5	12	7
Everton	5	2	0	3	9	6	6
Aston Villa	5	2	0	3	9	11	6
Nottingham Forest	5	2	0	3	10	12	6
Norwich City	5	1	2	2	8	9	5
Luton Town	5	1	1	3	11	14	5
Arsenal	5	1	1	3	4	6	4
Southampton	5	1	1	3	3	12	4
Ipswich Town	5	0	3	2	5	8	3
Birmingham City	5	0	1	4	2	17	1

Three points for a win, teams on same points separated by goal difference

Lion King

In a sense, the man who at the age of 16 fell in love with and subsequently married a teacher at his school has had many lives. In fact, Jenkins has started to write a reflection on those days and what to some would be a controversial romance. As they approach their golden wedding anniversary, he recalls with a smile when people said it would never work.

That is one of the fascinating aspects of his life, yet his post-Watford travails would be worth a biography in themselves.

He could have immersed himself in bitter reflections on the way his career at Watford ended and the wrangle over a diagnosis, but he tends even now to draw a veil over it all with a brief aside: 'It was not one of Dr Vernon Edwards' better moments.' Instead, Jenkins just got on with his life. Since Watford, he has played in Hong Kong and Cyprus; has joined and then owned a successful double-glazing business in Watford; emigrated to the USA and built his own house, with the help of a retired builder, by a lake in Michigan; become a bar and sports-complex owner in Javea; has spent months on safari in the true wilds of Africa over a number of years; helped work on a number of properties in Spain including a shepherd's cottage he owns up in the mountains, and more recently has written a couple of children's books. It has been a diverse life and Ross and Eve have enjoyed it to the full.

On being given a free transfer somewhat summarily by Watford, Jenkins was offered a better financial package by Howard Wilkinson at Sheffield Wednesday. 'I knew what he wanted me to do but I had to turn it down. Physically, with my injury, I was not capable of doing it. Had I been capable, I would still have been at Watford.'

Jenkins opted for a complete break with the English game when offered the chance to play in Hong Kong – the complete antidote to his disappointment. 'It was a very different, vibrant and energetic culture. It was fascinating. They offered me a lot of money and paid for the accommodation and flights. It was highly attractive and such a break from what I had been used to.'

During that time, Ross and Eve noted Elton John was to give a concert there, so they contacted the hotel and left a message.

'He came back almost immediately, invited us to the hotel, gave us concert tickets and dedicated a song to us at the concert. He was very warm and welcoming and we met his wife Renata and manager John Reid who, despite being a millionaire, was boasting about the bargain he had struck for a whole load of made-to-measure shirts.

'The Hong Kong experience did wonders for us drawing a line under Watford and English pro football.'

Jenkins started well, was able to ease into the less hectic schedule after 'building up effectively' in pre-season workouts. 'Then things began to fall away as a team and the owners looked to negotiate the end of your stay. I was paid up almost totally and I next accepted an offer to go to Cyprus. Well, that was a totally different environment from Hong Kong. There were a lot of spare hours in the day.

'I took my preliminary coaching badge and finished it in the UK after a chipped knee and an operation brought an end to my playing career.'

Their next decision was to do a 'world tour' of visiting friends but Jenkins hankered after a coaching post. 'I still felt I had something to offer the English professional game. We were back in Watford and when the coaching vacancies failed to come my way, I looked what else to do. Young Ross's education was stabilised and Eve became a teacher at Parmiter's, while I became a partner in a two-man double-glazing firm.'

He enjoyed a very brief coaching stint, training the strikers at Watford under Dave Bassett but the manager's full-time coaches objected to the appointment, so that avenue closed. When Steve Harrison was appointed manager, Jenkins offered to help as a coach but that also proved to be a dead end.

Jenkins took up golf – and he and I played regularly together – but when his father dropped dead three months into his retirement, Ross began 'to reflect on many aspects'. He had not anticipated his father's early demise. They had been close and he began to question whether driving round Watford's many roundabouts and fitting windows was truly what he wanted to do with the rest of his life.

He decided to move to Michigan, USA, for a year or so, having bought two plots of land with building permission by a lake. 'We built a house out in the wilds with the help of a retired builder. It was a fabulous three-bedroom house, with a mezzanine, a log fire and a large central area. We loved living there. Our son was at university out in the States.'

Jenkins learned to ski that winter – an easy transition for one who had sailboarded round Javea's bay for years – and they relished life among the moose and the occasional cougar.

Travelling up to Canada and then back to England in the summer, they were refused re-entry to the States on a technicality over which there was no appeal. They were forced to sell up their new house and the other plot of land and lick their wounds. Among the things lost in the turmoil was a framed dedication from Watford fans, presented at a special dinner.

'Throughout my life, when things have not worked out, I have moved on. I bought a three-bedroom house in Javea and played a lot of tennis. Then I was asked if I wanted to become a partner in owning a bar and sports complex. I did that for seven years. Sky TV came in at that time and, on football nights, we were packed. There was a pool, tennis courts, exercise room, fishing club, five-a-side court; it was absorbing but involved very long hours.'

Seven years later, Eve persuaded him to retire and they sold their interest in the complex.

'When I signed for Watford, we used the £1,000 signing-on fee to put down a deposit on an apartment in Javea. I came here for six weeks every summer while at Watford. We sold a house and the land in Michigan; we sold our house in Cassiobury, bought and sold a bar in Javea and now we have an apartment and we live in a three-bedroom house. Oh yes, and we have a two-room shepherd's cottage – a converted ruin in the *campo*,' he adds, using the Spanish term for countryside.

The cottage is in an idyllic situation with great views and they drive out to it regularly and enjoy the fact they are away from telephone and computer contact. Jenkins welcomes tranquillity; it is one of his favourite times. He is slowly developing the cottage because one of his traits remains – even as he approaches his seventies – in that he likes to be active. When he visits me, he insists I line up a project or work to do. Activity is his therapy.

Taking another break, they opted for a six-month safari in Africa and became hooked. They bought an old taxi, tent and camping equipment, which they keep stored in a garage in South Africa, with the car serviced every year. They adore tracking, watching and filming the wild life, and Eve has taken up photography with some award-winning results. They have a fund of anecdotes, such as waking one night to a funny smell and then realising a grown lion was standing the other side of the flimsy canvas. The lion roared repeatedly, the tent shook and finally the beast moved on, leaving gently quaking but relieved campers.

'You find yourself doing strange things that do not strike you as strange until you are back in Europe: such as following on foot, with the aid of a guide, a pride of lionesses on a hunting trip. We have gone back to Africa every year since, for four months, gradually reducing to our current two months. We are less adventurous now: we stay in designated areas in Kruger National Park instead of out in the wilds. Until recently we also went every winter for a month or two, renting a hut by the beach in Thailand.

'I retired from earning money at the age of 51. Apart from going to South Africa, we have very simple, relaxed tastes. I don't smoke; I drink a couple of beers, but I don't eat much either. I have had different lives involving dramatic switches, moving countries and houses. Eve has always been very supportive and we have been fortunate that my stepson John and little Ross fitted into our moves. Ross settled in Javea after

finishing university in the USA, has since married and we have
two grandchildren, and John loves the house and calls it home
when he visits.

'It has been such an active life, I wonder how I did it. The
most concentrated times were doing the windows, running
the bar and of course football at Watford. As a footballer, I
always believed in myself, was confident and a team player. But
now I look back on those days and am tempted to think it was
someone else.'

Returning to Watford – and feeling the 'tingle' on being
greeted by an ovation when he went out on the Vicarage
Road pitch – served to jolt those old memories. I returned to
him a collection of old scrapbooks he left with me when he
headed for Michigan and these, along with Graham Taylor's
death, funeral and most significantly the wake, have reminded
Jenkins that he did have another life and one that brought joy
to many people he has never met. The scrapbooks caused him
to ponder on how he managed to get his body in such unusual
situations. This volume of *Tales From The Vicarage* has also been
a trigger for the realisation that what he did at Watford from
1972 to 1983 actually mattered and was not just an interval in
his life but a melange of treasured memories for many people.

'Being remembered has made it all worthwhile. It seems I
had made my mark, which my dad always said was the aim. It
was the manager, the players and the whole crowd behind us.
It was a force of nature that made those times and it was very
special. It is nice to think it will always live on and be referred
to and that I was a part of it.

'It is only when you come out of it and then return, that you
realise how much football affects people's lives. Looking back,
and more recently seeing the fans, I am very glad I got on that
Watford train and made that memorable journey back to the
top flight. It seems we all made a difference.'

TALES FROM THE VICARAGE

Brilliant, original stories about Watford FC
by journalists, fans, former players and managers

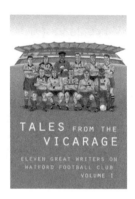

Tales From The Vicarage Volume 1

The first book in the series features former
Vicarage Road player David James, former
managers Brendan Rodgers and Malky
Mackay in addition to editor Lionel Birnie
and writers Simon Burton, Olly Wicken,
John Anderson, Adam Leventhal,
Andrew French, Tim Turner, Oliver Phillips,
Kevin Affleck and Stuart Hutchison.

Tales From The Vicarage Volume 2

The second book includes contributions
from former players Luther Blissett, Danny
Graham, Paul Wilkinson and Nigel Gibbs plus
editor Lionel Birnie and writers Mike Walters,
Andrew French, Ian Grant, Paolo Tomaselli,
John Murray, Adam Leventhal, Matt Rowson,
Olly Wicken, Miles Jacobson and Mike Parkin.

All books in the series are available now from
www.talesfrom.com

Tales From The Vicarage Volume 3: The Interviews

The third book is co-written by Lionel Birnie and Adam Leventhal and features interviews with eleven ex-Watford names – former managers Sean Dyche, Aidy Boothroyd and Ray Lewington and former players Craig Ramage, Nick Wright, Micah Hyde, Ronny Rosenthal, David and Dean Holdsworth, Tommy Smith and Paul Furlong.

Tales From The Vicarage Volume 4

Our fourth volume, edited by Lionel Birnie, features contributions from Troy Deeney, Marco Cassetti, Ikechi Anya, Jonathan Hogg, Fernando Forestieri, Tommy Mooney, Gifton Noel-Williams, Allan Smart and John McClelland.

Tales From The Vicarage Volume 5

Volume 5 comprises interviews with former managers Quique Sanchez Flores and Beppe Sannino and former players Tony Coton, Lloyd Doyley and Clarke Carlisle with contributions from editor Lionel Birnie and writers John Anderson, David Harrison, Stuart Hutchinson, Peter Jenson, Ciro Scognamiglio, Paolo Tomaselli, Kelly Somers, Olly Wicken and Mike Walters.

All books in the series are available now from
www.talesfrom.com